Stamp Collecting

A~to~Z

Stamp Collecting

A to Z

Walter Young

SAN DIEGO • NEW YORK
A. S. BARNES & COMPANY, INC.
IN LONDON:
THE TANTIVY PRESS

First Edition
Manufactured in the United States of America

For information write to:
A.S. Barnes & Company, Inc.
P.O. Box 3051
La Jolla, California 92038

The Tantivy Press
Magdalen House
136–148 Tooley Street
London, SE1 2TT, England

Library of Congress Cataloging in Publication Data

Young, Walter G
    Stamp Collecting, A–Z.

    1. Postage-stamps—Collectors and collecting.
I. Title.
HE6215.Y68   769.56'075   80-27181
ISBN 0-498-02479-2

2   3   4   5   6   7   8   9   84   83   82

Acknowledgments

I am indebted to several philatelic experts and specialists who supplied factual information for various parts of this book. They include Jack Williams of the Philatelic Information Branch of the United States Postal Service in Washington; Franklin Bruns, Jr., of the Division of Postal History, Smithsonian Institution; R.G. McKee and Adrienne Bérubé of the Public Affairs Branch of Canada Post in Ottawa; Jeanne D. Mears of *Linn's Stamp News*; Lorne Bentham and Bill Olcheski of *Stamp Collector*; and Jerome Husak of the American Topical Association Inc.

In certain related areas—financial, technical, aesthetic, for example—I also received authoritative help from contacts in pertinent fields: stamp dealers and auction houses, insurance and security people, papermakers, printers, layout artists.

The reference numbers given parenthetically throughout with individual stamps are all Scott Catalogue Numbers, and are used with the permission of the Scott Publishing Co.

W.Y.

Contents

S tamp collecting, to put it in simplest terms, is the happiness of pursuit. It's also the happiness of concocting exactly what you're going to pursue.

A stamp club in our town allows each member a twenty-five-word statement in its roster to describe his interests and wants. The club is big as stamp clubs go, with over a hundred members—enough to be generally representative of what collectors like to collect. And you need read only a few of the members' statements to see how diversified stamp collecting—philately—can be. Strongest interest is predictably in individual countries, especially the United States and Canada, and topical themes come next. Then in the area of what might be called creative specialization is revealed one of philately's fundamental attractions: the unlimited subjective possibilities it offers. Take these four members' statements of interest, each quoted word for word:

Retired plant foreman: "All foreign stamps honoring American people, places, history, I mount them with the U.S.A. stamp on the same subject."

Housewife: "Stamps with outdoor pictures from any country as I make my own albums showing only scenery— must cost 3¢ or less."

High school student: "All airmails from every place even Iron Curtain if you have."

Newspaper reporter: "My collection is titled 'One World.' I want any country's issues on the subject of international cooperation, projects, conferences, games, etc."

So here are four dissimilar people—a retiree proud to be American, a thrifty housewife with an eye for the scenic, a teenage flying buff, a diplomacy-minded newspaperman—all enjoying philately's happiness of pursuit, but each pursuing his own personally devised specialty.

But the chance to be innovative is only one reason for stamp collecting's worldwide popularity. Consider its simple but strong basic attractions. Stamps are easy to collect, being such readily available everyday items. They are attractive and colorful, featherweight and compact. They are automatically and painlessly educational. And collecting them ranks with the least expensive of hobbies.

It is true that there are hundreds and hundreds of stamps far out of the financial reach of the average collector, including some that only the wealthy can afford. But it is also true that out of some 200,000 recognized varieties there are thousands and thousands so common that they will never cost more than a few cents each; you can spend a lifetime pursuing only those. There is so much penny material around from all eras as far back as the mid-nineteenth century that many a large and satisfying collection has been built out of little else. You can buy in packets for under twenty dollars almost half of all the U.S. stamps ever issued, and for under ten dollars almost half of all the Canadian stamps; or for around thirty dollars you can obtain almost 5,000 different worldwide issues, enough for perhaps a couple of years of pleasurable sorting, identifying, and mounting. And the collector who has more than a minimum to invest regularly in filling spaces can add innumerable important and storied stamps to his albums, even without getting into extravagant costs; an example is the famous world's first stamp, Great Britain's Penny Black of 1840, still often available used at under a hundred dollars—not a trifling outlay, to be sure, but one that would be considered nominal in many hobbies.

Of the many kinds of accessories available only a very few are actual necessities for anyone but the advanced specialist or philatelic scholar. Everyone should have a perforation gauge, magnifier, watermark tray, and tongs, but you can buy all these items together for under five dollars. Everyone must have an album, but you can buy adequate albums for a few dollars (and of course you can spend a lot more if you want something more detailed and capacious). Some of the numerous other accessory items are equally inexpensive and a few can be helpful, but all are discretionary for the intermediate general collector.

In handling stamps you can't help learning, among other things, something about history, geography, and notable people from many fields. Franklin D. Roosevelt considered stamp collecting an important contributor to his knowledge of the world, and Britain's King George V once said that since his duties mostly kept him close to home, working with stamps was substitute travel for him.

With so much to offer it's hardly surprising that stamp collecting has long been considered the world's leading hobby. Some educated estimates of recent years place the worldwide number of collectors as high as 30 million, with over 10 million of them in the United States and Canada; the figures are approximate because they're necessarily based partly on deduction, but there seems no reason to doubt their plausibility—if anything, they're possibly conservative. Philately has been a favorite relaxation of countless celebrities including royalty, heads of state, writers and composers, musicians, entertainers, athletes, and high-ranking servicemen and churchmen. And it has been a lifetime hobby of untold millions of us ordinary people.

There are a few old familiar tales about the origins of stamp collecting. It started, so one story goes, soon after the original Penny Black was issued, even while the Black and its two-penny counterpart were still the only two stamps in the world to collect. Fashionable London ladies began gathering canceled copies of the stamps, both of which bore the head of the young Queen Victoria, for decorating their tableware and bric-a-brac. Their pursuit became such a craze that in 1842 it prompted from the British magazine *Punch* a remark so often quoted that it's almost legendary, "The ladies betray more anxiety to treasure up Queen's heads than Henry the Eighth did to get rid of them." Another often-related incident from the era concerns the young woman who advertised for bulk quantities of canceled stamps for an unusual purpose; she wanted them as wallpaper for her bedroom. Whether she received enough to complete the project is not recorded, though it seems unlikely she did—even for a single wall only ten feet long she would have needed over 16,000 stamps. That could be a reason why some historians claim the ad was a hoax, placed by an opportunist who planned to start the world's first stamp dealership with the free merchandise it netted him.

In 1852 or thereabouts, as a way to make geography more interesting, a schoolteacher in Belgium started his pupils seeking stamps for mounting on their atlas pages. Since by then there were around thirty-five issuing countries or territories, that was probably stamp collecting's true beginning. About a decade later a group of French collectors provided the first categorizing of stamp features and details, the first catalogs and albums appeared in various places including the United States, and in Brussels the first stamp dealer opened shop; so scarcely twenty years after the first stamp was issued the new hobby was firmly established. One contemporary English authority wrote that the collecting of stamps would some day prevail as a hobby over the collecting of birds' eggs, a prediction that doubtless brought comfort to incalculable mother birds throughout Britain— and of course quickly turned out to be true.

II

Around the turn of the century major topics of debate in the United States Congress concerned the possibility of building a canal from ocean to ocean through the Central American isthmus and the route such an undertaking should follow. A canal had been started by France several years earlier, but the project was abandoned because of engineering problems and the decimating effects of yellow fever among the workers. France's attempt had been made through Panama, which was then part of Colombia, and for the United States to continue the same route seemed the obvious choice. But considerable opinion favored starting afresh through the narrow southern neck of Nicaragua, partly because the French interests wanted something like $75 million more for their Panamanian rights than Congress was willing to pay. Then, as a stalemate loomed, a set of postage stamps helped decide the matter.

Promoters of the Panama route armed themselves with a quantity of current Nicaragua stamps showing the active volcano Mount Momotombo, a Nicaraguan landmark, and sent some to each voting legislator. The implication was clear: Choose the Nicaragua route and you can expect to contend with volcanic eruptions both when building the canal and when operating it, adding to the ever-present problems of sanitation and disease. When the vote was won by the Panama supporters it was close—so close that it's reasonable to credit the Nicaragua issues with helping to influence a history-making decision.

On two occasions stamps showing incorrectly drawn maps have been the cause of international skirmishes or border wars in Latin America (see Mistakes on Stamps: Dominican Republic, Nicaragua),* and an Estonian set of 1936 commemorating Saint Briggita's convent is said to have so infuriated Stalin that it helped stimulate his plan for having the USSR swallow up Estonia, which had outlawed communism in 1924; in 1940 he accomplished the plan when Estonia was taken over by Soviet forces on trumped-up charges.

Stamps have been officially used as money at times as far back as the Civil War, when in 1862 and 1863 the U.S. Treasury Department issued cards printed with stamps to be used as scrip during a coin shortage. About the same time stamps were frequently encased in metal capsules by business firms for the same purpose. The many other examples of stamps as money include those in Europe during and after World War I, when several countries utilized them encased or printed on cards, sometimes to meet a currency shortage but often to serve a more vital purpose; the stamps replaced coins made obsolete by runaway inflation, and without them day-to-day retail business might have been almost impossible to transact.

As all stamps except the plainest definitives publicize somebody or something, they are an obvious and ready medium for propaganda. Happily, only a few countries with little philatelic repute capitalize on the opportunity to any great extent; blatant proselytizing is usually avoided in the issues of most countries. An effective example of brainwashing by government did occur, however, in Egypt in 1953. After Farouk was deposed as king in 1952 the reform regime overprinted past issues bearing his portrait with

---

*All parenthetical references are to headings in the Encyclopedia/Reader section.

heavy black bars defacing his features. A complete new stamp issue had been brought out after the takeover, but the regime wanted to emphasize its contempt for Farouk by giving wide circulation to his obliterated picture. The action was an effective piece of propaganda that helped ensure the new government's permanence.

An incident reported around 1885 in a British periodical even links stamps with classic literature. In the early 1860s near the English city of Oxford, a little girl was running across a field with a handful of used stamps for her book when she tripped and let them flutter away. A few landed in a rabbit hole, prompting her to wonder out loud to one of her father's friends who was nearby what she would see in the hole if she went down into it after them. The friend was Charles Dodgson, and while the story may be apocryphal, the fact is that when in 1865 his book *Alice's Adventures in Wonderland* appeared under the pen name Lewis Carroll, Alice's adventures started, as everyone knows, when she descended into a rabbit hole.

But the true role of stamps in history has been their effect on communication. In less than a year after the world's first stamp was introduced in 1840 in Great Britain to replace the cumbersome method of postage payment in cash by sender or recipient, the volume of mail more than doubled (see Penny Black). During the next several years, as other countries began issuing stamps, mail grew worldwide at an astronomical rate. The convenience of the postage stamp encouraged people to keep in touch with relatives and friends, allowed extension of business operations, facilitated international congress. And as the use of postage stamps grew, so did the number of stamp collectors; and as the number of collectors grew, so did the number of stamp-issuing entities who saw in them an exploitable market.

III

Before the nineteenth century ended, stamps issued primarily for collectors while filling no real postal requirement were starting to appear. Sometimes they consisted of complete regular issues, sometimes only of unneeded high denominations; commemoratives were still largely undiscovered as sources of extra revenue. A few minor states were also learning that the tail could profitably wag the dog and began producing stamps primarily for the philatelic market, with issues and printing quantities out of all proportion to the relatively modest postal needs of their scanty populations. Altogether, though, the overwhelming majority of nineteenth-century stamps were legitimate issues; exploitation of collectors didn't become significant until after World War I, or really flagrant and widespread until after World War II.

Today new issues are constantly being offered almost solely as collector material (see Wallpaper). Moreover, several small states of otherwise good repute have practically become philatelic factories to the point where an important part of their revenue is dependent on the stamp trade. They're easy to identify; when you see new issues continually coming from a state with a population of only a few thousand people, you can be sure the stamps are produced mainly for collectors, not to meet any true postal need. Yet there is no reason why you shouldn't collect such stamps if you want to. Certainly for the most part they're colorful and attractive—you just have to remember that they'll never have any particular value.

Even some of the most philatelically respected countries occasionally or frequently come out with stamps whose only justification seems to be their profit-making potential. The United States is sometimes guilty of this; in 1978, for instance, many people including noncollectors failed to see how a country-music singer could warrant a commemorative. Other issues of the same year that drew adverse reaction included the quilt and dance sets, making 1978 an average twelve months—every year, it appears, has its share of stamps whose subjects seem to have been chosen almost at random and not because of any true merit. In Canada there was wide unfavorable sentiment regarding the multiplicity of sets marking the 1976 Olympic Games held in Montreal; the first Olympic stamp came out in 1973, and by the time the last appeared in 1976 there were a total of thirty-six varieties, including the country's first semipostals (see), commemorating the Games, which despite their international flavor don't merit that many stamps except as revenue-producing collector material.

It's to be hoped that the increase in recent years of the use of lightweight, nonsignificant stamp subjects is only a faddish trend that will some day be halted. The least desirable result of the trend is its weakening effect on one of philately's top fringe benefits, the painless—even pleasurable—education it affords. Practically every stamp-issuing country must boast enough noteworthy people, memorable places, and history-making events to allow it to produce meaningful stamps almost indefinitely. Stamps devoted to things like love symbols, ice-skate cartoons, or children's balloons—to pick a few topics that have been used—have little more significance than colored labels and are hardly likely to win commendation from either postal patrons or collectors.

Another growing practice of recent years has been the issuance of stamps in se-tenant form. Se-tenants consist of two or more varieties in groups with each other on the same full pane (see Se-Tenant). They may be mainly a way of promoting the sale of blocks instead of single stamps; and since se-tenant singles by themselves are almost invariably of regular letter-rate denomination, blocks have minor postal application and used ones are likely to have been canceled to order (see Canceled to Order). If no more se-tenants were ever issued, few collectors would mourn.

In a different vein , it's hard to equate the homely look of many of today's stamps with the increasing sophistication of printing processes and presumably of design skills. While admittedly the aesthetics of classic stamp design and relief-printed engraving have been almost entirely supplanted by modern ideas and techniques, there can be little reason for the undistinguished look of the U.S. Americana series, for the kindergarten-poster appearance of the U.S. energy stamps of 1977 with their heavy-handed artwork and color, or for the overall unattractiveness of the U.S. 1976 Interphil issue; or for the uninspired 1972 bicycling issue of Canada (which additionally was a trivial commemorative subject to begin with). These few ugly ducklings are merely typical, and not necessarily the worst, of the disappointing issues that emanate now and then from almost any country.

IV

Yet there's a brighter side. While unneeded issues, unpopular formats, and unhandsome designs have existed for years, taken all together they still make up only a fraction of the thousands and thousands of varieties available for the pleasure and edification of collectors. Meaningful subjects artistically presented do abound among the issues of the great majority of countries.

The United States has produced numerous stamps of uncommon distinction. After more than eighty years the 1898 issue commemorating the Trans-Mississippi Exposition is still widely considered one of philately's most aesthetically pleasing sets. The Presidential definitive series of 1938, by chronologically showing all U.S. presidents from Washington to Coolidge along with their dates in office, provides a palatable history lesson; and its single chaste design and bust portraits are a striking example of classic simplicity and one reason it remained current for sixteen years. The multidesign Liberty series, which in 1954 replaced the Presidentials, includes fifteen stamps of identical pattern showing either a president or some other American personage; these fifteen, too, are in simple good taste and among the most attractive of U.S. stamps (see Omahas; Presidentials; Liberty Issue). The Bicentennial four-stamp Contributors to the Cause set of 1975 is a well-executed example of full-color design, and in addition calls attention to four lesser-known heroes of revolutionary times. All of these, moreover, are just a selection of the many U.S. stamps that have won admiration over the years.

Canada, too, has an overall record of high standards in its stamp-issuing programs, the following being only a few random examples. The ever-popular Diamond Jubilee series of 1897 used only one design for all of its sixteen varieties, but the set has always been a favorite with collectors and the design repetition has never seemed to hurt its desirability (see Diamond Jubilee). The various high-denomination definitives issued during the reign of George V and illustrated with Canadian places and other Canadiana are for the most part both prepossessing and popular, qualities reflected in the increasing demand for some of them. The provincial issue of 1964 giving each province and territory an individual stamp showing its coat of arms and flower met early resistance among some collectors who felt the series served no needed purpose; nevertheless it soon gained desirability because of its unpretentious but refreshing design. And the trim little low values of 1977 colorfully featuring indigenous wildflowers are surely among the most attractive definitive stamps issued by any country in recent years.

Numerous countries in Europe can claim a record of consistently judicious stamp-issuing policies. Examples include Finland and Norway, both of which have maintained quality while exercising some restraint in quantity. Liechtenstein has been almost alone among the tiny states and duchies in holding down its number of issues to something in keeping with its small population and consequent limited postal needs, and as a result its stamps have always been well regarded among collectors. But the country enjoying the longest-lived collector esteem is Great Britain, which with few exceptions was always philatelically conservative and only during the latest several years has stepped up its issuing rate—well over half of all the country's stamps are of the reign of Queen Elizabeth II. Although of good repute, Great Britain stamps for more than a century were utilitarian or even dull, but that's no longer true. Today the commemoratives are almost invariably handsome and interesting, and the long single-design definitive series in use since the country's conversion to decimal currency at the end of 1970 is pure classic treatment of the queen's head. All British stamps are further enhanced by the small neat perforations traditionally used on them.

Throughout the rest of the world are similar examples of philatelically respected countries; they can largely be identified right from a catalog because as a general rule they're the ones whose stamp subjects have some degree of national significance and whose issues are not excessive in number. For the most part, British Commonwealth countries rate well in these criteria, which is one reason their stamps are popular among collectors.

While several references above sound like arguments for moderation in the number of stamps a country issues, the fact is that there is no wide agreement on whether fewer stamps really would be a desirable change. Those favoring present levels contend that most collectors today limit themselves to one or a few countries, and need frequent new issues to keep their pursuit challenging. It can be pointed out, too, that the U.S. State Flags issue of 1976, with fifty different stamps to a pane, was strongly criticized by many individuals and most philatelic organizations as being exploitation; yet it was greeted with immediate and heavy collector demand, and few issues of recent years can match its investment potential (see State Flags Issue). Although there is little doubt that stamp overabundance hurts a country's credibility, collectors, generally speaking, seem satisfied with the numbers of new issues that keep coming out. And of course nobody is ever forced to collect anything he doesn't approve of.

All things considered, it isn't hard to see why the many attractions of stamp collecting are more than enough to outweigh its occasional trivialities—and why stamp collecting is likely to remain the great worldwide hobby it has been for over a hundred years. It's fascinating to realize that any stamp we place on a letter we mail could end up some day, somewhere, as someone's admired possession—the prize that puts the happiness in the pursuit.

2
User's Guide

This book is designed to provide reference and how-to information for general stamp collectors, especially for collectors of United States and Canadian stamps. To accomplish this it embraces an encyclopedia and reader along with two general-interest list sections as follows:

Encyclopedia/Reader (**section 3**). To keep the book compact and to the point, the subjects covered in this section are for the most part well within the overall objective. Some marginal ones were omitted if they seemed not really relevant and in addition were adequately handled in other publications with different slants—perhaps broader slants, or conversely, more specialized ones. Omissions include, for example, details on foreign stamp identification, rundowns on stamp-issuing countries (but section 4 is a listing of international philatelic agencies), currency tables, and because of the book's generalist viewpoint, highly specialized treatises. Careful selection of subject matter has also produced a corresponding opposite benefit, the space to include many long comprehensive articles like those on such general subjects as stamp condition, mistakes in design, topical collecting, and notable rarities; on such instructive subjects as how to distinguish paper types and printing methods, how to protect collections against theft, and how to create pleasing album pages and exhibition frames; and on such financially oriented subjects as insuring collections, selling collections, and avoiding the pitfalls of stamps as investments.

For verity, many of the articles were developed with the help of related experts—layout artists, printers, insurance people, to name a few—besides the several philatelic authorities consulted as needed. The result is a body of information much of which is not likely to be found in comparable form in any other published source, but which is information of significance to the general collector, the one to whom this book is addressed. In addition, and also in keeping with the book's slant, there are frequent references to United States and Canadian philatelic matters including individual stamps. And a specially devised two-part, cross-referenced index system (following in this section 2) allows quick locating of any covered subject, either by looking it up alphabetically or by checking the subject's basic category.

Stamp identification numbers shown in parentheses in encyclopedia listings are Scott Catalogue Numbers, and are used with the permission of the Scott Publishing Co.

Philatelic Agencies by Country (section 4). While it is generally accepted that nine of ten United States and Canadian collectors collect the stamps of their own country, fewer than half of them collect their own country exclusively. For this reason—particularly for those collectors who wish to keep up with new issues in foreign stamps—this section is devoted to the mailing addresses of the official retail philatelic agencies of practically all stamp-issuing countries. Also given here are tips on dealing with these foreign agencies, which in many cases present language barriers or unfamiliar business methods.

Topics for Topical Collecting (section 5). Topical collecting being possibly the most popular sideline of general collecting, a long list of collectible topics and subtopics is provided in this section. The list is also a demonstration of the multiplicity of subjects treated on stamps, making it of potential interest to philatelic students as well as a source of suggestions for general collectors looking to take on a new pursuit.

Two-Part Encyclopedia Index System

Index I: Alphabetical

Note that this is mainly an alphabetical listing of subjects in the same order in which they appear in the encyclopedia/

reader, to provide a fast convenient means of checking subject content especially when a subject might be called by more than one name.

An asterisk preceding the listing indicates that the article contains specific United States or Canadian mention: a stamp or stamps, or other reference, however brief.

Index II: By Category

Use this index for locating article headings by their general category, and also for ascertaining all the article subjects in a given category. Often a subject obviously belonging in one classification has secondary significance in another, in which case it is listed in both; for thorough cross-referencing, this practice is followed even when the secondary connection is almost negligible. (Note that for fullest presentation of a subject there is also a good deal of cross-referencing in the encyclopedia entries themselves.)

A typical example of the utility of this classified index is the category Care and Handling of Stamps, which lists over a dozen pertinent articles that taken together embrace just about all aspects of stamp care, including some that if not mentioned might not be thought of in connection with the subject, like the one on color cancellation; but this article contains an important caution on preventing stamp damage. Similar useful cross-references occur throughout most other categories. Finally, it should be noted that some article subjects do not fit into any collective category, and consequently appear only in the alphabetical index and not in this one.

The index contains twenty categories, covering basically all matters of interest to the general stamp collector. They are as follows:

17. *Rarities*

Acquiring Stamps. The various sources and methods for accumulating stamps and building collections are described under their alphabetical headings throughout this book. For bulk quantities of heavily duplicated used stamps still on paper, see Mixture, Bank Mixture, Mission Mixture, Kiloware. For packets of all-different stamps ready for mounting, see Packets and How They Are Priced. For individual stamps, see Approvals, Auction, Circuit, New-Issue Service.

Adhesives. Describes gummed stamps as distinguished from nonadhesive stamps printed directly onto such items as envelopes, letter sheets, and postal cards. Adhesives on or off cover are the stamps of interest to the general collector, nonadhesives usually being collected as specialized material.

Admirals. Popular name for the 1912–26 definitive issues of Canada showing King George V as an admiral in Royal Navy uniform.

Aerogram. A lightweight letter sheet designed to be folded to form its own envelope, for use as an international airmail letter. When of government issue the stamp is printed on the sheet. Aerograms are collected as specialized material.

Aerophilately. The collecting and study of airmail stamps and other airborne postal material. This extensive branch of philately has its own specialized clubs, organizations, and literature.

GEORGE V ADMIRAL

Air Cover. An envelope or other postal wrapper bearing airmail stamps, an air label (see), or other evidence that it was postally forwarded by air.

Air Label. Any label affixed to an envelope or other postal wrapper instructing air forwarding. The standard air label of Universal Postal Union countries is blue with white letters in both the language of the issuing country and French, the latter being the official language of the UPU. The familiar French air-label phrase *Par Avion* means *By Plane*.

Also see Universal Postal Union.

Airmail. It is natural to think of airmail as always having gone by plane, as it does today. But the first official airmail flight was by balloon. It was in 1859, when John Wise (who in 1858 had ballooned 800 miles from Saint Louis to northern New York State) took off from Lafayette, Indiana, in his balloon *Jupiter* with mail addressed to New York City, 700-odd miles away. Weather conditions forced him down in nearby Crawfordsville after only twenty-five miles, but the flight was considered significant enough to be noted at its centennial in 1959 with a U.S. commemorative airmail stamp (C54).

Other early balloon mail flights were attempted with mixed success in Tennessee and in several places in Europe, with some degree of regular scheduling being achieved in at least one case (see Balloon Mail).

What is believed to be the first airmail trip by plane took place in France in 1908, less than five years after the Wright brothers flew successfully at Kitty Hawk. Letters were carried from Paris to Saint Nazaire, a distance of 225 miles. Many experimental flights followed throughout the world during the next few years, until World War I intervened. But soon after the 1918 armistice several international airmail routes were operating in Europe, their distance limited to a few hundred miles by the aircraft of the time.

Airships were used as carriers during their short heyday in the 1930s, until the *Hindenburg* disaster in Lakehurst, New Jersey, in 1937 signaled their commercial demise. They were too slow to be much more than a novelty in any case, especially with the flying range of planes continually increasing.

Airmail's growth following World War II was accompanied by an abundance of airmail stamps from most countries; a notable exception is Great Britain, which has never issued airmails. Airmail stamps have always been among practically every country's most colorful and interesting emissions, good reasons for their steady popularity with collectors.

United States. Regular airmail service in the United States predated World War I armistice by six months, having been inaugurated between Washington, Philadelphia, and New York in May 1918. The first U.S. airmail stamps, a set of three, were issued during the same year. In 1934 an airmail special delivery stamp appeared, combining the fees for the two fast services; two years later this stamp was superseded by a second, more colorful one (CE1–CE2). Due to minor public interest in the stamp, it was in use only a few years. By the mid-1970s air service was automatic for most first class intercity mail, and all airmail stamps were discontinued except for the overseas denominations. By 1977 there were ninety airmail varieties, including the coveted three-stamp Graf Zeppelin set (C13–C15) and the storied and rare 1918 invert (C3a) (see Zeppelins; Rarities: U.S. Inverts).

Canada. For many years following World War I, airmail was handled by private aviation companies, delivering mainly to remote areas. Government service began in 1928 and the first airmail stamp was issued the same year. There had been a government-authorized stamp produced in limited quantity in 1927 in connection with an ill-fated flight from London, Ontario, to London, England; it is extremely rare, and because it was not strictly an official issue, it is uncataloged (see London-to-London Flight Stamp). Airmail special delivery stamps appeared in 1942, and in contrast to the U.S. experience were used extensively. Both types of stamps were phased out in the 1950s when they became redundant as first class intercity mail was gradually switched to air carrier. There are nine airmail and four airmail special delivery varieties, none of any great scarcity; in addition, three of the regular issues of the 1950s were intended mainly for airmail, although not so indicated on the stamps (313, 320, and 343).

Album. The first stamp albums appeared around 1862. The original one was published in France in three language editions—French, English, and German—and was worldwide in scope, as were the several that soon followed in

Europe and America. Then in New York in 1868 the first country album was published; it was for the stamps of the United States, of which by that time there were around one hundred including variations and minor varieties.

Today, from the handful of major U.S. and Canadian publishers alone, there are almost two hundred different albums for collectors to choose from. They include world-wide albums, and albums for individual countries or groups of countries or for such other collectibles as covers, blocks (see both), full mint panes, and postal stationery. They come bound or loose-leaf with pages printed or unprinted, and in some cases consist of more than one volume. With so many variables to consider, selecting the right album for your own needs becomes a matter of careful evaluation and comparison.

Choosing an Album. The beginning collector may well start with a bound album with printed pages for stamps of the world. It will be arranged by country and contain spaces for most of the commonest varieties and a few blank spaces for new issues. It will be of some value to the beginner, if only in helping him learn to identify stamps' countries of origin. But since at best it will hold only a few thousand of the two hundred thousand or so cataloged varieties, it will quickly be outgrown.

Loose-leaf albums, printed or unprinted, are the only practical ones for the intermediate collector. Those with printed pages have an allotted space for each stamp, or are a combination of allotted spaces and blank discretionary ones. They vary from one another mainly in page design—a matter of personal preference—and more important, in the number of stamps they allow spaces for. If you're an average-hobbyist kind of collector, an album that's too complete for you will forever show many unfilled spots, sometimes pages of them, a condition that emphasizes what you don't have instead of what you do have; on the other hand, you want an album complete enough to have a space for every stamp you're ever likely to acquire. So if you prefer a printed album, your choice should be decided largely by your philatelic goals. The album should have pages printed on one side only, and it should offer supplement pages for each year's new issues.

Unprinted albums come either with perfectly plain pages or with feint-ruled quadrille pages, the latter used to help achieve balanced, plumb layouts. Because of the freedom they allow in page arrangements and in treatment of specialty material, unprinted pages are the type generally used by advanced collectors, specialists, and those who exhibit in stamp shows.

Hingeless albums, as their name implies, hold and display stamps without the use of hinges. Various methods are used to accomplish this, including transparent pockets and overlays. Hingeless albums are used mainly by advanced collectors, are comparatively expensive, and in some collectors' opinions have two drawbacks: They make it harder to inspect stamps closely and they cut off much of the air circulation that is generally considered beneficial to stamps.

Most loose-leaf albums are either ring or post-and-hinge types. With all of them, ordinary loose-leaf reinforcements are recommended for the page holes. Reinforcements protect the holes against tearing; in addition, by adding a layer of paper at the holding points, they eliminate bulge when the thickness of stamps is added to the page.

Also see Laying Out Attractive Album Pages; Writeups and How to Prepare Them.

All-Americans. Early popular name for the U.S. 1902–3 definitive series (300–313) carrying portraits of Americans prominent in various fields, and featuring the first of several appearances of Martha Washington on U.S. stamps. Nicknamed after the All-American football selections which had been started a dozen years earlier, the issue has always been a collectors' favorite largely because of its baroque designs, a distinct change from the severe unadorned portraiture that had been used on almost every previous U.S. definitive series.

ALL-AMERICAN

Americana Series. A U.S. definitive issue with a Revolutionary Era theme introduced in 1975 as a short series and expanded from time to time over the next few years with additional values (1591+). Except for one multicolor, each stamp carries a simple illustration in a single color on a plain unframed background on colored or off-white paper. The stamps are not handsome, especially compared to present-day foreign and other U.S. emissions, and give little indication of attaining wide collector popularity.

American Bank Note Company. Printers of early postage stamps including the U.S. issues of 1879–88 (182–245) and the Canadian issue of 1859 (14–19), and of occasional later U.S. issues starting with the Overrun Countries series of 1943–44 (909–921), the first U.S. stamps printed by a private company since the Bureau of Engraving and Printing took over stamp manufacture in 1894.

Also see Bank Note Issues; Bureau Prints.

Aniline. A chemical found in many industrial products including some of the inks formerly used in printing postage stamps. Aniline inks are soluble in water, so older stamps possibly aniline-printed should not be soaked to remove paper; instead they should be carefully floated off the paper or treated in a humidifier.

Also see Removing Paper from Stamps; Humidifier.

A Percevoir. (French) to collect. The phrase has appeared on Canadian postage-due stamps since 1933, and also appears on postage-due stamps of France and French colonies (see Postage Due).

Approvals. Priced stamps mailed on a speculative basis by dealers to customers, the customer keeping those he wishes to buy and returning the rest. Stamp collecting is particularly suited to this method of buying and selling, because stamps are light and compact to mail—a single ounce can contain over 150 varieties—and because the customer is able to give careful study to his purchase before buying, an essential step because of the importance of condition in judging a stamp's value. Thus approvals are popular with dealer and customer alike.

While often sent out in random assortments, approval shipments are more satisfactory when made up by the dealer following his customer's stated needs, general and specific, as outlined on a want list (see). They are sometimes sent automatically on a continuing basis, in accordance with such other customer instructions as frequency of shipment and maximum total value per shipment (although there is never customer obligation to buy any stamp from the lot).

To become an approvals customer consult the philatelic newspapers and magazines, where large numbers of mail-order dealers are represented by ads offering selections to specialists and general worldwide collectors.

Archer Perforations. The first postage-stamp perforations, made experimentally on stamps of Great Britain starting in 1848 by Henry Archer, inventor of a perforating machine. By 1853 the process was considered workable and the British post office bought Archer's machine and patents. The following year the post office began issuing the country's stamps perforated.

Arches. Popular name for the 1930–31 definitive issues of Canada showing King George V below a curved frame resembling a rounded arch. While these are the only issues to be so called, the 1928–29 series had also shown the king under an arch, a different style known as a segmental arch.

As Is. A condition that indicates serious defects in a stamp's condition. Stamps so described are sold without return or refund privileges.

Auction. Apart from being a principal method of selling stamps in quantity, auctions are important in setting actual market prices; realized auction amounts often vary considerably from the listed catalog values that in many cases are necessarily theoretical, especially in the case of rarities.

Auctions may be conducted live or by mail, or they may be a combination of the two with mail bids being entered by agent at the proper stages of floor bidding. At any given time there are several forthcoming auctions accepting mail bids, and catalogs are always available on request.

The catalogs list and describe in standardized terms every stamp to be offered, usually picturing many of them; catalogs are sent to interested collectors, often for a nominal charge as they are costly to produce, in advance of the closing date for bids. While each lot goes to the highest bidder, in mail auctions it is not necessarily for as much as the bidder was willing to pay; most auction houses require only a nominal advance over second high, and thus a successful bidder may take down a lot for a price less than the full amount of his offer. Rules on credit, return privileges, misdescription, and similar details vary from auction to auction, and are outlined in the catalog.

To obtain auction catalogs consult the philatelic newspapers and magazines, where auctions are advertised and editorially listed.

av, ave, avg. Average (see).

Average. A grade of stamp condition. For definition of recognized grades, see Condition.

Back of Book. A collective term meaning all types of postage stamps except regular issues; it takes in airmail, special delivery, official, and the other categories found on the back pages in printed country albums and at the end of a country's section in catalogs. The term commonly appears in its abbreviated form, *B.O.B.*

Backprint. Anything printed on the back of a stamp. Backprinting has occasionally been used in a pattern of fine lines or dots as a device to discourage forgery.

An early example of backprinting as part of the stamp design was the 1895 Portuguese set of fifteen values commemorating the seven-hundredth anniversary of the birth of Saint Anthony of Padua (132–146), each stamp containing a Latin inscription on the reverse. U.S. examples of backprinting are on the ten-stamp Postal People issue of 1973 (1489–1498) and the four-stamp Contributors to the Cause issue of 1975 (1559–1562), in both of which each denomination carried short text on the back relating to the picture on the front. There are no backprints on Canadian stamps.

There have been experiments—all of them short-lived— in using backprints for advertising messages. Advertising appeared on some copies of the Great Britain penny value of 1881 and halfpenny of 1887, and some 1882–95 issues of New Zealand. Postal use of the backprinted Great Britain stamps was forbidden, and none are known in used condition; it was allowed in New Zealand, and used specimens, although not common, are favorites with many collectors. In both cases the backprinting merely adds interest; none of the stamps are separately cataloged varieties.

Backstamp. A postmark on the back of a piece of mail. Backstamping is no longer common practice, but at one time it was widely performed in many countries for various purposes, the most common being to mark incoming mail at receiving post offices along the forwarding route. Backstamps are of interest to collectors of early covers, being important in the study of routes and elapsed times.

Balloon Mail. After a first abbreviated attempt at forwarding mail by balloon in Indiana in 1859, there were a number of recorded instances in both America and Europe into the early twentieth century, but none were successful enough to trigger regular service. During the siege of Paris in 1870 in the Franco-Prussian War, however, manned balloons were used several times to take mail out of the city. Because the flights were made under wartime conditions they had no degree of regularity. There is no record of any return flight making it back into Paris, although some were planned; undelivered covers exist that would have been carried. Covers from the outbound flights are prized by collectors of such material, particularly those bearing the inscription *Par Balloon Monte (By Mounted Balloon)*. Balloons were also used to carry pigeons out of Paris to Tours, where the pigeons were fitted with messages and released to fly back to the besieged city.

Also see Airmail; Pigeon Post.

Bank Mixture. Unsorted mixed stamps still on paper and sold in bulk, so called because they're made up largely from the incoming mail of businesses including banks. Bank mixtures are assumed to contain good proportions of high-denomination domestic and foreign stamps, and thus are considered worth more than mission mixtures (see) containing mostly everyday low values.

Bank Note Issues. Popular name for the U.S. issues of 1870–88, so called because they were printed by three different bank-note companies in succession: National Bank Note Co., Continental Bank Note Co., and American Bank Note Co. The latter two merged in 1879 and continued in business under the American name. In 1894 the Treasury Department took over the printing of U.S. stamps, and no more were privately printed until 1943 (see Bureau Prints).

Bars. Commonly used in overprinting on stamps, bars are the usual means of blocking out the former value when an existing stamp's denomination is changed. They usually appear as heavy black short horizontal lines. They have been used occasionally by some countries to void stamp remainders sold to the philatelic trade, a practice that reduces collector value of the stamps so treated. Other of the various purposes served by bars have included government self-promotion, as in 1953 when they were overprinted on Egyptian stamps by the new reform government to further discredit the deposed, unlamented King Farouk by disfiguring his face.

In the United States and Canada lighter bars extending across a stamp's width are the devices used for pre-cancellation.

BASEL DOVE

1859 BEAVER

Also see Overprint; Precancel.

Basel Dove. Popular name for the 1845 stamp (3L1) of the Swiss canton of Basel, showing a dove within a decorative escutcheon. Printed in black, crimson, and blue, it was the world's first tricolor stamp. It was in service for only a limited time and is relatively scarce.

Batonné Paper. See Paper Types and How to Distinguish Them.

Beavers. Popular name for four early Canadian stamps depicting the beaver, a national symbol. They were issued between 1851 and 1859, one of them being the country's first stamp as well as the first stamp in the world to show an animal. In 1951 the original design was reproduced on one value (314) in the set commemorating CAPEX, an international philatelic exhibition.

Bicentennial, Bicentenary. A two-hundredth anniversary, a frequent occasion for a commemorative stamp. The American Revolution Bicentennial in 1976 was the most widely commemorated one in stamp history. The first U.S. stamp to mark it (1432) was issued in 1971, well in advance of the bicentennial year, and showed the symbol of the official Bicentennial Commission; many more appeared during the next several years, the issues reaching their peak in 1976 and continuing for further years. In 1976 Canada commemorated the U.S. bicentennial with a ten-cent stamp showing Benjamin Franklin (691), as did many foreign countries with a variety of issues.

Bicolor. A stamp printed in two colors, a type uncommon enough to be of special interest before multicolor printing presses came into general use starting in the late 1950s. The first U.S. bicolors appeared on the higher values (118–122) of the definitive series of 1869, the next in the 1901 Pan-American issue (294–299), and the next on the five-dollar value (573) in the definitive series of 1922, after which they appeared spasmodically until the 1950s when they became common. The first Canadian bicolors appeared on the 1898 Imperial Penny Postage issue (85–86), and the next in 1939 on the set commemorating the royal visit (246–248); they also started becoming common in the 1950s.

Bilingual. In philately, a stamp bearing two languages. Canadian stamps have been printed bilingually—English and French—since 1927. Canada also issued the world's first stamp printed in three languages; see Trilingual.

Compare Bilingual Pair.

Bilingual Pair. Two adjoining stamps printed in different languages. Common examples are the many South African issues before the mid-1950s in which English and Afrikaans were alternated on the stamps in a sheet. Thus one stamp would read SOUTH AFRICA and the one next to it SUID-AFRICA.

Bisect. A stamp cut in half, each half being worth in postage half of the complete stamp's denomination. In early stamp-issuing days and during war years bisecting sometimes used to be authorized to overcome a shortage of a particular value, or to reduce the post-office inventories of a value. To be accepted as authentic, bisects must be collected on cover. There are no official U.S. bisects.

In Canada the Port Hood Provisionals of 1899, while not strictly bisects, served the same general purpose. There were two of them (88b, 88c), both cut from the same Queen Victoria three-cent value, one being a third of the stamp with an over-printed 1 over the numeral 3, the other one two-thirds of the stamp with a 2 overprinted on the numeral. Their values were one cent and two cents, and they are rarities not recognized by all catalogs because they were not officially authorized.

PORT HOOD PROVISIONAL

Black Jacks. Popular name for six U.S. two-cent stamps of 1861 and later (73+), black in color and bearing a portrait of Andrew Jackson after a miniature by J. W. Dodge. The stamp's design was unusual for U.S. issues of the time because of the large size of the portrait, which occupied almost all of the stamp but the corners and made the subject's face appear to be coming right out of it. Black Jacks are favorites among collectors of U.S. stamps, although some are quite expensive and none are less than several dollars apiece.

BLACK JACK

Blackout Cancel. A postmark with the name of the town removed, used in Canada in areas near the seacoast as a security measure during World War II to keep servicemen's outgoing mail from disclosing their location and movements.

Block. A rectangular group of unseparated stamps with at least two in each horizontal and vertical row (if in a single row, unseparated stamps more than a pair are known as a strip). Blocks may be several stamps in each direction but are always less than a full pane.

Collected blocks usually contain the minimum of four stamps two by two, very often with the adjoining margin unremoved because of the information printed on it: plate numbers or other printing controls, mailing instructions, or slogans. Sometimes to carry all the plate numbers shown on the margin requires several stamps horizontally or vertically. In se-tenant stamps, blocks containing all varieties are generally of substantially higher value with or without margins than the total of the individual stamps when separated; se-tenants are groups of different stamps printed on the same pane, usually four together but sometimes two or three.

Also see Pair; Strip; Plate Block; Corner Block; Se-Tenant.

BNA. British North America (see).

B.O.B. Back of book (see).

Bogus. A completely fraudulent stamp, not to be confused with a fake, which is a genuine stamp that has been altered to deceive in some way, a facsimile, which is an admitted likeness of a stamp, or a counterfeit or forgery.

A bogus stamp is either an entirely fictitious issue of a real country or an entirely fictitious issue of an entirely fictitious country. At one time stamps in such bogus monetary units as kroden and ruples from such bogus countries as Martania and South Niger, and frequently bearing equally bogus postmarks, used to crop up periodically. But bogus stamps are not seen as often today, largely because the plethora of stamps emanating from many countries makes the printing of fictitious stamps unprofitable. Some of the stamps from these prolific countries have bogus characteristics themselves, even if not technically, in the sense that they were issued primarily to take money from collectors instead of to serve as postage.

Also see Fake; Facsimile; Forgery.

Bond Paper. See Paper Types and How to Distinguish Them.

Booklet, Booklet Pane. Booklets of stamps were introduced in 1895 by Luxembourg as a convenience to postal patrons, a useful idea that was soon adopted by other countries. The collecting of booklets and booklet panes is a popular specialty, some of the early booklets now being rarities. For album display, booklets are usually exploded—that is, freed of staples and separated page by page—and all pages including covers individually mounted.

A booklet pane is an individual page from the book, generally consisting of six or fewer stamps. Normally the edges of a booklet pane are trimmed to the stamps, meaning that all stamps on the pane have at least one straight edge, the two outside corner stamps having two adjoining ones; this distinguishes booklet stamps from coil stamps (see), which have two opposite straight edges.

In the United States a few stamps have been issued in booklet and coil forms only and not in regular full panes with perforation on all sides; examples are the eight-cent rose-violet Eisenhower of 1971 (1395, 1402) and the thirteen-cent Liberty Bell of 1975 (1595, 1618).

Bourse. An organized assemblage of dealers forming a market or fair for buying and selling stamps. A bourse is usually sponsored by a stamp club or dealer group, and is almost invariably one of the activities at stamp exhibitions.

At all times price variances are normal from dealer to dealer, some of them caused by subjective opinions in grading stamps. For this reason it can be profitable to shop when buying or selling, and by having many dealers assembled in one place bourses make comparison shopping easy. They are mostly held weekends with free admission in public halls or hotel meeting rooms, and are frequent in metropolitan areas and not infrequent in many smaller towns, some being periodic affairs at monthly or other intervals. Bourses are listed in the philatelic publications and sometimes in local newspapers; in addition, local stamp dealers can tell you about any bourses being held in your area.

Brilliant Mint. Describes a stamp of early issue in perfect mint condition, distinguishing it from early mint stamps of average condition, which can show color fading and other slight imperfections.

British Colonials. Loosely describes the stamps of the British Commonwealth of Nations (see) and British dependencies. The term is somewhat inaccurate, since many members of the commonwealth have not been classed as colonies for decades.

British Commonwealth of Nations. A political association of nations comprising Great Britain and the former British dominions and dependencies. Commonwealth stamps, including the present remaining dependencies, are widely collected as a body, as are the stamps of certain geographical groups within the commonwealth, notably British Europe, British North America (see), British Oceania, and British West Indies. Popular specialties are the commonwealth omnibus issues, made up of commemoratives from many of the countries on a single topic, the topic often being an important event in the life of the Royal Family.

British North America. A philatelic group consisting of Canada and the former stamp-issuing entities that are now Canadian provinces: New Brunswick, Nova Scotia, Prince Edward Island, British Columbia, Newfoundland, and Vancouver Island (now part of British Columbia).

Bull's Eye. Popular description of a cancellation or postmark perfectly centered on the stamp, also colloquially described as socked on the nose. Some collectors and philatelic organizations make a practice of placing stamps on envelopes toward top center instead of in the usual top right-hand corner, to favor gaining a bull's-eye postmark from the canceling machine. Although canceling machines don't position exactly, in the United States a reasonably well centered town-and-date circle postmark should result if the center of the stamp is about 3¼" from the envelope's right side and about ⅝" from the top; in Canada the distances are about 3" and ½".

Bureau Prints. Stamps printed by the U.S. Bureau of Printing and Engraving, the first of which were the definitive series of 1894 (246+), when the Treasury Department took over stamp manufacture from the private bank-note companies. The government did not return to private firms for stamp printing until the Overrun Countries issue of 1943–44 (909–921), which was produced by the American Bank Note Company, printer of U.S. stamps from 1879 to 1888, to take advantage of the company's multicolor process. A few other U.S. issues since then have also been printed by private companies.

Also see Bank Note Issues.

Cachet. A decorative or promotional design appearing on an envelope or other postal cover, usually to mark an occasion that has philatelic significance. Such occasions include a stamp's first day of issue, a first airmail flight, historical anniversaries, philatelic exhibitions, and similar happenings. Most of today's cachets are commercially produced for mass sale, or privately produced to mark club events. Although cacheted covers are widely collected, cachets basically add visual interest only; because they are common and have no philatelic purpose, they don't increase a cover's value.

Also see First Day Cover; Mulreadies.

Camels. Popular name for a long-lived series of definitive stamps of the Sudan, showing a letter carrier riding a camel. The illustration was introduced in 1898 on the first Sudanese stamps, and except for a few years in the 1940s appeared on every definitive value until 1951, when it was mostly superseded by entirely new designs but still retained on one value. In 1948 at its fiftieth anniversary it was the subject of its own commemorative (95), and it reappeared in 1954 on a three-stamp set (115–117) marking the start of Sudanese self-government.

CAMEL WITH OFFICIAL OVERPRINT

Canada Post. The Canadian post office department and its philatelic branch. The latter offers new-issue subscription and other services to collectors. Address: Philatelic Service, Canada Post, Ottawa, Ontario K1A 0B5.

Canal Zone Errors. For the first thirty years of the Canal Zone's existence under U.S. jurisdiction the stamps of the zone were those of the United States or the Republic of Panama, overprinted CANAL ZONE. Starting in 1904 over a hundred stamps received the overprint, and on many of them it is found in any of a variety of errors: printed upside down or double, or with one word missing, or with the two words reversed, or in other incorrect configuration. The numerous affected stamps are mostly scarce individually.

Cancellation. The lines or other markings placed on a stamp to prevent its reuse. The term is used interchangeably with postmark, although some philatelists prefer to limit it to the part of the mark that cancels, and the postmark to the circle or other device that contains place name and date. The cancellation is colloquially known as the killer, an expression originally used to describe early markings, such as those from cork cancelers, that were heavily defacing.

Early Canceling Experiments. For decades after adhesive postage stamps first came into general use, an official fear in stamp-issuing countries—apparently justified—was that larcenous people would use the same stamp over again unless it were subjected to some form of cancellation to make reuse impossible. This fear led to innumerable canceling proposals, some of them bizarre. Most were never seriously considered, for which today's collectors can be grateful; had they been adopted, the supply of nineteenth-century used stamps would have been significantly lessened.

Proposals included tearoffs, cutouts, and disfigurements by such instruments as saws, cutters, hole punches, and roughing rasps. One inventor even suggested branding the stamp with a miniature branding iron. A main reason for the rejection of many treatments, apart from impracticality, was that they would have wrought equal harm on the envelope and its contents.

An idea briefly tried was a half-inch window cut into the envelope, the stamp covering the opening and sticking to both envelope and inside letter, causing it to be ruined when the letter was removed. Another, unadopted, was a stamp made to come apart in several pieces once the gum was used, so there was no way to remove it whole from its cover; it would have been a forerunner of today's unswitchable retail price tags that can only be pulled off the merchandise in pieces.

Tearoff suggestions were common, a typical one proposing half-gummed stamps so the canceling clerk could simply tear away the unstuck half. They too were considered impractical, except very briefly in one or two Asian countries.

Modern Canceling Practices. Fortunately machine canceling arrived before the end of the nineteenth century, and since its inception heavy disfiguring markings have mostly come through postal services where hand stamping is frequent or customary, like parcel post—which means that higher values are proportionately more defaced than everyday ones. Generally speaking, though, all countries today cater to collectors and for the most part provide philatelically acceptable cancellations. ·

In the United States and Canada, and in most other countries, the envelope receives the place-and-date postmark to the left of stamp position, with killer lines or a slogan canceling the stamp. Cancellation collectors and others who want place and date to appear on the stamp often position the stamp on the envelope at the spot where it is most likely to be struck with the postmark instead of with canceling lines; the approximate spot for this is given under Bull's-Eye (see).

Special cancellations for events and commemorative stamps are available to collectors in the U.S. and Canada, as well as in most foreign countries, and so are special canceling arrangements through temporary philatelic post offices at stamp shows. Such offerings appear regularly in stamp publications and newspaper columns, or you can contact the postal services of most countries direct; addresses are given in section 4 of this book, "Philatelic Agencies by Country."

Also see Postmark; Cork Canceler.

Canceled to Order. Describes stamps canceled in quantity by the issuing country without going through the mail, for sale to the trade as used stamps. Stamps are canceled to order for any of several reasons: to reduce a country's mint inventory, to dispose of mint remainder stocks, to create a supply of apparently used stamps from countries too small or too uncultured to produce enough postally used ones, or to fill wholesalers' orders. From this it's obvious that canceled-to-order stamps are much less desirable than those that have actually passed through the mail, but for the collector needing used varieties to fill album spaces they are sometimes the only ones available. Stamps canceled to order are usually not hard to identify; very often the mint adhesive remains on the back, and the cancellations themselves can generally be spotted as imitations.

Strictly speaking, the stamps on individually canceled unaddressed covers are canceled to order, although they're not widely admitted to be so; but the fact is that they receive a cancellation without having served any postal purpose, just as the stamps do that are canceled to order in bulk.

In recent years in the United States, canceling to order has been done on postage-due stamps to increase the supplies available for collectors, as many post offices now use meter tapes instead of stamps to indicate postage due. Needless to say, this practice is not welcomed by collectors.

The term canceled to order often appears in its abbreviated form, cto.

Also see First Day Cover; Postage Meter.

Carriers' Stamps. Until 1860 the postage stamps of the United States covered only the forwarding charge from one post office to another; delivery to the addressee was done by private local carriers, who also handled whatever intracity mail didn't have to pass between any post offices. To facilitate fee payment the government issued official carriers' stamps in a few cities and authorized unofficial ones in several others; catalogs list about sixty emissions for Baltimore, Boston, Charleston, Cincinnati, Cleveland, Louisville, New York, Philadelphia, and Saint Louis. None of the carriers' stamps are common, and a few are rarities.

Also see Locals.

Catalog. A general worldwide reference catalog comprises one or more volumes listing by country all recognized postage stamp varieties in every type of stamp, with identifying number, picture, value mint and used, and other information. A catalog is an indispensable tool for the collector, being the basic guide to intelligent accumulation and organized arrangement of stamps from anywhere in the world. Several major catalogs are published in America and Europe, most of them annually, a few at more frequent intervals. Many thousands of changes are made in them from year to year, involving both price adjustments and the addition of new stamp emissions; in recent years the latter alone have been numbering well into the thousands.

Catalogs also give such particulars as date of issue, color, perforation size, method of printing, paper variances, watermark data, and any other details needed for stamp identification or study. Despite all these specifications, however, differences between some stamps are so slight or so hard to recognize that the average collector cannot be positive in his identification of them. This is a common problem, but for anything except run-of-the-mill stamps, where even the nominal fee wouldn't be justified, it can be solved by calling on an expertising service, which will supply documented identification (see Expertising).

A stamp's catalog number is the way the stamp is universally identified for buying and selling, but numbering systems differ from catalog to catalog. In the United States and Canada the generally accepted identifying numbers are those given in the Scott catalogs. Scott is also foremost for cost reference, although other catalogs are sometimes used for this purpose; some philatelists feel that Scott prices are not entirely true market reflections, since the publisher is not a stamp dealer as well. Other U.S. catalogs include the worldwide Minkus and the smaller Harris, which embraces only the United States, Canada, and the United Nations. The publishers of both are also dealers, so their catalogs are actually their price lists and therefore presumably more realistic as to market values. In Canada, Lyman's catalog of British North America is widely used in pricing, although it also is issued by a nondealer publishing house.

Stanley Gibbons is the predominantly used worldwide catalog in the British Commonwealth outside of Canada; it has been published in London since 1865, making it the oldest existing catalog, and it appears in multiple versions and sections. Other major foreign catalogs include Yvert & Tellier (France), Michel (Germany), Zumstein (Switzerland), and Bolaffi (Italy).

There are other general catalogs in various languages, and numerous specialized ones of interest only to the philatelists in the fields they serve. Finally there are the countless dealer catalogs of stamps and supplies, and the auction catalogs continually being issued, both of which are mentioned only because they are also called catalogs; they bear no relationship in format or purpose to the general reference catalogs.

Catalog Value. Stamp values given in a general reference catalog are seldom actual market prices unless the catalog is also the publisher's selling list, which is not the case with Scott, the most widely used catalog. In many instances Scott prices are primarily a guide to relative values and a starting point for actual pricing; no stamp is shown at less than a few cents, for example, although thousands of them are sold universally for under a penny apiece. It should also be noted that catalog values are theoretical prices at which the stamps can be bought, not an indication of what the stamps will bring if the collector sells them; the old schoolboy habit of toting up catalog values of all stamps in an album to establish the collection's worth is pure delusion.

Despite all this, philately would be a chaotic pursuit without the influence of catalog values. Some dealers do sell all except the commonest stamps at Scott prices. More of them sell at a fixed percentage of Scott; "50% of Scott" (or 25%, or 33%, or 60%) frequently headlines dealer ads. Many sell specific numbers at an advance over Scott, believing certain catalog values to be unrealistically low. Extra-fine condition can also command a premium over catalog price. But in all cases the catalog value is the basis that makes reasonable pricing possible, allowing the collector to shop with greater confidence than he could if he didn't have it to serve as a yardstick.

The term catalog value commonly appears in abbreviated form, cv or c/v.

Catapult Mail. For a few years starting in the late 1920s while planes were still too short-range to fly oceans nonstop, France and Germany experimented with catapulting mail planes from ships at sea. The planes were able to land while the ships were still several hundred miles out of port, speeding mail by as much as a day. Most pieces of catapult mail were identified with a special cachet (see).

Centennial, Centenary. A one-hundredth anniversary, an occasion often marked with a commemorative stamp. Centennial issues are common in both the United States and Canada. The first in the United States was the Louisiana Purchase set of 1904 (323–327), the first in Canada the 1933 stamp noting the first transatlantic steamboat crossing (204).

Centering. The position of the printed area of a stamp within its margins, a perfectly centered stamp being one with equal margins all around. Most modern stamps are reasonably well centered, if not always perfectly so; earlier ones are sometimes badly centered, even to the degree of having the design cut into by perforations. Centering is an important factor in determining a stamp's value.

Also see Condition.

Certified Mail. Mail for which the post office gives the sender a receipt and obtains from the addressee a delivery receipt. Certified mail provides evidence of delivery only, at a lower fee than registered mail; it provides no insurance against loss, as registered mail does. A single certified mail stamp was issued by the United States in 1955 (FA1) and discontinued two years later, although the service remains.

Chain Breakers. Popular name for several 1919–20 stamps of Yugoslavia, and several 1920–25 stamps of Czechoslovakia, showing symbolic figures breaking their chains of bondage. In both countries the reference was to their emergence as independencies from the ruins of the Austria-Hungary monarchy when it was dismembered at the end of World War I.

Chalk Lines. Intersecting chalky lines underprinted on Russian stamps in 1909 as a short-lived experiment in preventing the removal of cancellations. Any attempt at cleaning the stamps would wash away the chalk lines and consequently the printed matter over them.

Chalky Paper. See Paper Types and How to Distinguish Them.

Chalons. Popular name for three Canadian stamps issued between 1851 and 1859 (3, 9, 18) bearing the Alfred Chalon full-face portrait of Queen Victoria. The first stamp is a well-known rarity and was reproduced in 1978 on a twelve-cent CAPEX issue (753). The Chalon portrait, a famous one, was the first done of the queen after her accession in 1837, and was used again by Canada—but turned right to left—on the Diamond Jubilee issue of 1897 (50–65). It also appeared on all the stamps of New Zealand from the first issue in 1855 until 1872 (1–49), but was never used on any Great Britain stamp. An original engraving of the portrait published in 1838 is in Canada's National Postal Museum in Ottawa.

Also see Rarities: Canada Twelve-Pence Chalon.

Also see Rarities: Canada Twelve-Pence Chalon.

1857 CHALON

Changeling. A stamp whose color has changed due to age or exposure, or has been changed chemically for fraudulent purposes.

Charity Stamp. See Semipostal.

Christmas Stamp. A stamp with a religious or secular Christmas theme, sold for a limited time primarily for use on Christmas mail but valid for any regular postage. Many countries issue Christmas stamps, which have appeared annually in the United States since 1962 and in Canada since 1964. Despite their limited sale duration in both countries, most except a few Canadian higher values are plentiful. The two 1898 world-map varieties of Canada (85–86) show the inscription XMAS 1898, and hence are commonly referred to as Christmas stamps; officially, however, they were the Imperial Penny Postage issue.

NON-CHRISTMAS

Christmas Toys. Popular name for the se-tenant four-stamp U.S. Christmas issue of 1970 (1415–1418 and precanceled 1415a–1418a) which showed an old-fashioned child's toy on each stamp.

Circuit. A system for buying and selling stamps by mail within a closed group, in which the stamps for sale travel a prescribed route among the group. A circuit is often an activity of a club, open to members of the club and administered by a sales committee. Typically, members with stamps to sell mount them in books and price them, and the committee assembles several books into a circuit package and sends the package out on its rounds. Each member of the circuit keeps any stamps he wishes to buy, puts his mark in their place, remits payment to the sales committee, and forwards the package to the next name on the list. When the circuit is completed the package comes back to the committee, who audit the sales records and make payment to the sellers, less a commission for the club.

Usually circuits consist of eight to twelve members and are arranged so that members move up in order as each new package is sent out; thus each member has a turn at being first to receive a package. Circuits can contain general or specialized material, some large clubs having numerous types making the rounds at all times. Similar groups within local organizations have the advantage of being able to circulate the stamps without using the mails, saving both postage and insurance costs as well as time.

U.S. CLASSIC FIRST ISSUES

Classic. A classic stamp is one distinguished by its beauty or rarity, or in some cases by an interesting or unusual history. It must also be old, but there is no general agreement on how old. Some philatelists feel a classic should be pre-1870 or -1875, two of the years frequently and somewhat arbitrarily mentioned as dividing lines; others are in favor of a specific age, one hundred years being commonly proposed.

U.S. classics include the first two stamps issued (1–2) and the Black Jacks of 1861–75 (73+). Canadian classics include the early Prince Alberts (2+) and the first Queen Victoria Chalon (3). Because of their great popularity, however, most nineteenth-century stamps of both countries, except the repetitious ones, are close to classic status.

Also see Black Jacks; Chalons.

Cleaned. Describes a stamp from which a cancellation or other postal marking has been removed for a dishonest purpose, usually philatelic. The term does not apply to a stamp legitimately cleaned of dirt or stain to improve its appearance. A used stamp cleaned and reglued can often be passed off as mint at many times the used price, although experts have various ways of detecting such alteration.

Cleaning Stamps. See Renovating Soiled or Damaged Stamps.

Cogwheel Punch. An embossing performed by small punches arranged in a circular pattern, used experimentally on U.S. stamps in 1873 as a means of preventing removal of cancellations; the punches crushed the paper fibers, making them absorbent to cancellation inks.

Also see Grill.

Coil Stamps. Stamps issued in single-row rolls called coils, for use in dispensers and vending machines. In the United States and Canada coil stamps are separate cataloged varieties because of their easily distinguishable perforation differences, the perforations appearing only on two opposite sides. They are frequently collected in pairs, which some feel demonstrate the coil format better than singles—a debatable point.

Also see Line Pair.

COIL PAIR

Collateral. Related material displayed with collections or stamps on exhibit pages to provide documentation or other detail. Collateral material can include illustrations, news items, maps, charts, or anything else pertinent. In most cases it should be used sparingly, and only to further the presentation—it should not assume greater importance than the stamps it supports.

Color Cancellation. While most postal cancellations are black, cancellations in red or purple or occasionally other colors are sometimes seen. Color cancellations were used more often in early times than they are today, when they were usually the result of handstamping. They are often soluble in water or other liquids, so as a general rule color-canceled stamps should not be soaked to remove paper or subjected to watermark-detecting liquids.

Also see Removing Paper from Stamps; Watermark Detecting.

Color Change. A stamp's color may be changed by the issuing country for any of various reasons. Many changes were made throughout the world in 1898, when agreement was reached by member countries of the Universal Postal Union (see) to have standard colors for the three values heavily used in international mail; the one-cent, two-cent, and five-cent denominations, and their approximate equivalents in other currencies, were to be green, red, and blue respectively. But over the years conformance wasn't invariable, and the agreement was brought to an end in 1953, partly also because due to changed postage rates the values it covered had become of minor importance internationally. Another instance of major change was in Great Britain in 1941–42, when colors were lightened on the six low values of the George VI regular issue as a wartime measure to conserve ink chemicals.

Except for two in 1898 to conform to the UPU agreement, there have been no U.S. color changes on individual stamps. In Canada there was one for UPU conformance in 1898, and there have been subsequent ones on issues of George V, George VI, and Elizabeth.

Color Guide. A printed folder or printed cards showing and naming colors that appear on stamps, used mostly by specialists for identifying minor shade varieties. A color guide may illustrate 150 or more shades. It should be used with judgment; color nomenclature is not always identical among catalogs and other reference sources, colors on stamps sometimes fade or otherwise change with age, and the same color can appear different on different papers.

COLUMBIAN

Columbians. Popular name for the 1893 U.S. issue (230–245) commemorating the World's Columbian Exposition, which was held that year in Chicago to mark the four-hundredth anniversary of Christopher Columbus's discovery of America. The issue consisted of sixteen values bearing Columbus-related scenes and portraits, and although they were the first commemorative stamps ever in the United States, they were not entirely well received. Many people including nonphilatelists objected to the high values from one dollar to five dollars, which were not postally needed, ninety cents having been the highest previous denomination. There was also concern about a supposed blunder, the fact that the one-cent value showed a clean-shaven Columbus in sight of land while the two-cent value showed him landing on San Salvador a day later with a full beard. But although inconsistent, this was not a blunder; it was simply that the two scenes were taken from paintings already existing, as were most of the illustrations in the series. The Columbian stamps were largely neglected for decades, but since World War II interest in them has steadily increased and so has their value, in some cases many times over. Today they are among the most popular U.S. issues and are likely to become even greater favorites as we near the Columbus quincentennial in 1992.

Columbus has appeared on many stamps throughout the Americas, but never on a Canadian stamp. He was shown on a dozen or so varieties of Saint Kitts-Nevis between 1903 and 1922 in what is probably the best-known anachronism in philately (see Mistakes on Stamps: Saint Kitts-Nevis)

Column. For convenience in locating stamps on a sheet, column usually means vertical, and row, horizontal.

Combination Cover. A cover bearing stamps of more than one country. Combination covers were common before the Universal Postal Union (see) was established in 1874, because international mail normally required postage in both sending and delivering countries.

Comb Perforation. A type of perforation accomplished by a device that punches the holes in the general pattern of a comb, one straight row across the full width of a pane of stamps as well as the vertical separations between all the stamps in the row. Thus at one time it perforates three sides of each stamp in a single row.

Commemorative. A stamp that in addition to prepaying postage honors a person or place, commemorates an anniversary, marks an event, or publicizes an organization or cause. As a general rule commemorative issues are on sale for only a limited time, theoretically making them likely to increase in value at a faster rate than definitive stamps (regular issues); but since today's commemoratives are normally printed in huge quantities, this seldom happens any longer. Commemoratives are popular with collectors if only because of the extra interest generated by their subjects, as well as by their usually larger size and colorful designs.

The 1871 issue of Peru marking the twentieth anniversary of South America's first railroad (19) is generally accepted to be the first true commemorative stamp. Today thousands of new commemoratives are issued throughout the world every year, many of them intended more for sale to collectors than to serve a postal need. In such emissions comparatively few of the stamps ever become postally used, which is why some commemoratives are priced higher in used condition than in mint.

Commercial Overprints. Starting in the mid-nineteenth century in Great Britain, transaction receipts for over two pounds were taxed a penny, which in 1920 was raised to two pennies until the tax was abolished in 1971. In 1881 postage stamps became valid for payment of this tax. This meant that major retail establishments carried large stamp inventories for their receipts, leading to pilferage problems. To prevent these problems the government allowed firms to overprint the stamps, the overprint usually taking the form of the company name and sometimes words like *Paid* or *Received.* While officially these overprints were not valid for postage, there are many examples on cover of them postally used.

Commonwealth of Nations. See British Commonwealth of Nations.

Competition Exhibiting. Entries in competitions held by clubs, stamp shows, or exhibitions consist of pages of stamps and other philatelic materials displayed under glass in frames that in most cases—but not invariably—hold six standard mounted pages. An entry usually requires a few or several frames, meaning a dozen or more pages, to present adequate development of its theme.

In creating pages for exhibiting in competition, the accepted guidelines for layout and notation should be followed (see Laying Out Attractive Album Pages; Writeups and How to Prepare Them). In addition, competition entries have specific characteristics of their own. Some vary with the competition and are spelled out in the rules for the event. Others are of a general nature and are outlined below. If there are differences between rules and generalities, the former take precedence.

Preparing Exhibits. The first page should give the title, along with a brief introduction elaborating on the title and indicating how its theme will be presented. Stamps may or may not appear on this page. A catchy title adds interest, but it should also be reasonably self-explanatory. To illustrate one simple way to build an exhibit on the subject of U.S. states:

Show each state in order of its admission to the union, possibly being introduced by its stamp from the State Flags issue of 1976 (1633–1682) and detailed by one or more additional stamps commemorating something about it or a person associated with it. To add a distinctive touch indicate each state's capital city with a precancel (see) bearing the city's name, or with a postmark from the city cut out square and mounted on the page like a stamp. Many other inclusions are admissible as long as they are pertinent to the overall theme. A title and introduction to such an exhibit could go something like this:

AS 13 BECAME 50: THE FIRST 169 YEARS

The states of the union with their capital cities, in the order of their admission from the original 13 in 1790 to the 50th in 1959, and a sampling of how they've been remembered on stamps: their people, their achievements, their historic milestones.

The introduction page could be completed with two stamps, one showing the original thirteen-star flag (1622) and one showing the fifty-star flag (1153 or 1208).

Because exhibition frames display all mounted pages simultaneously, competition entries require another consideration, one that's relatively unimportant for album pages viewed consecutively: Exhibit pages not only must be pleasingly laid out individually, but they must be laid out with good relationship to each other. This means that a single page with a purposely unsymmetrical layout would probably distract in an exhibit otherwise containing only balanced layouts; equally important, it means that there should usually be no great diversity in the quantity of material appearing from page to page.

Depending on the nature of the competition and the theme of the entry, acceptable material for an exhibit can include postal stationery, special postmarks and cancellations, local issues if valid for postage, and similar philatelically sound items. Material to be avoided includes wallpaper (see), commercial postcards unless postally used, and labels and other nonphilatelic items. And it's particularly important that nothing appear that cannot be related to the exhibit's theme or fitted into its organizational plan; in the states exhibit outlined above, for instance, the Erie Canal commemorative of 1967 (1325) would be admissible as a New York achievement, but the Arkansas River Navigation issue of 1968 (1358) would not be admissible because it cannot be related just to one single state, the river being important in four different ones.

Most competition experts consider the material itself to be the truly significant part of any philatelic exhibit, with presentation—the matters discussed here—of less importance. This opinion is not universal, however, and in any case a clean, attractive, and imaginative but meaningful presentation should always be an exhibit goal. A good presentation cannot do anything but enhance a competition entry; a poor one cannot do anything but detract from it.

Protecting from Theft. Under today's conditions of increasing home break-ins and burglaries, it is advisable to omit your name entirely from exhibit pages, or to use a nom de plume. It's equally important not to accept publicity if your exhibit receives an award. For other tips on providing for the security of your stamps, see Protecting Stamp Collections from Theft.

Compound Perforation. Differing perforation sizes on the same stamp, the perforations on top and bottom being in one gauge and on the sides in another. Compound perforations have appeared on many stamps of the United States and Canada.

Condition. The state or quality of a stamp, a major determinant of its value. The usual classifications (superb, very fine, fine, etc.) are used by some to refer only to the centering of the stamp's design within the perforations. Others prefer condition to take into account such additional matters as the degree of color retention; the state of the paper, perforations, and gum (if unused) or cancellation (if used); and defects like tears, pin holes, and thin spots, if any. The latter approach is shared here; it seems the more practical one for both buyer and seller since it results in an overall evaluation.

A stamp graded superb can bring a premium over catalog value, and one graded average will probably be available for less than catalog value. Many earlier stamps are graded against the average for their issue and described accordingly, some issues being generally of higher quality than others; thus one stamp may be graded fine for its issue while another of similar condition but from a different issue is graded only fair for its issue. Condition is a necessary part of a stamp's listing in catalogs of auctions or mail sales. Because much depends on personal judgment, stamps that appear practically identical may be graded differently by different dealers, and consequently priced differently—a good reason for comparison shopping when buying stamps of more than small cost.

74

Condition Designations and Details. The generally accepted grades of stamp quality are basically as follows:

SUPERB: flawless in every respect including centering, color, gum or cancellation, perforations or imperforate margins; and free from any defect. (This term is used primarily in describing nineteenth-century stamps.)

VERY FINE: close to superb, especially in centering and gum or cancellation.

FINE: nicely if not perfectly centered, nicely canceled, other qualities at least good.

VERY GOOD: possibly off center, possible medium–heavy cancellation, other qualities at least good.

GOOD: probably off center, heavily canceled, or with minor defects, but of reasonably good appearance.

AVERAGE: probably off center and heavily canceled, and usually with some defects as well.

FAIR, POOR: much like average, but with some damaging defects.

SPACE FILLER: badly enough damaged to be barely worth keeping, but sometimes used as a temporary filler for an album space.

Most of the above designations appear, often in abbreviated form, as shown next along with many of the frequently used terms for describing other details of condition. The few terms that need additional explanation are in most cases discussed in their own separate alphabetical headings throughout this book.

av	average
ave	average
avg	average
cp	clipped perforation
cr	crease
cto	canceled to order
def	defects, defective
f	fine
g	good
hc	heavily canceled
hh	heavily hinged (on unused, means gum disturbed)
hr	hinge remnant (usually on unused)
lc	lightly canceled
lh	lightly hinged (on unused, means gum marked)

m	mint
mc	medium cancellation
ng	no gum (on unused)
nh	never hinged (mint)
og	original gum (on unused)
perfin	perforated initials
ph	pin hole
prec	precancel, precanceled
rg	regummed (on unused)
rp	repaired
se	straight edge
sp	short perforation
sup	superb
th	thin, thin spot
tph	tiny pin hole
tr	tear
tth	tiny thin
ttr	tiny tear
u	used (also frequently indicated by a dot within a circle)
un	unused (also frequently indicated by a star or asterisk)
vf	very fine
vg	very good

Note that some dealers may use additional classifications and terms, and some may have slightly different interpretations of classification meanings from those given here. This needn't confuse, however, since a catalog or other sale offering usually carries an explanation of its own terminology.

Confederate States of America. During the Civil War the Confederacy issued its own stamps starting in October 1861. The stamps made a unique contribution to American postal history by depicting C.S.A. president Jefferson Davis, who appeared on eight of the fourteen varieties and thus became the only person ever to appear on an American stamp during his lifetime. In addition, one of the values—the 1862 five-cent blue (6)—was first printed in England; it was the only U.S. stamp ever printed outside the country. None of the C.S.A. stamps are particularly common, a few being scarce and one or two being rare.

Also see Confederate States Provisionals.

Confederate States Provisionals. Stamps and envelopes issued by local C.S.A. postmasters mostly between June 1861, when U.S. stamps became invalid in the Confederacy, and October 1861, when the Confederacy's own stamps were introduced; the provisionals also appeared at other times during the Civil War to meet the stamp shortages that sometimes occurred. The postmasters of forty-three towns in nine Confederate states issued stamps; almost twice that number issued envelopes recognized by catalogs, although in many cases they were simply ordinary envelopes hand-stamped with the local post office's cancellation. All of the issues, both stamps and envelopes, are rare, some of them extremely so; there is only one known copy of the five-cent red-brown stamp of Mount Lebanon, Louisiana (60X1).

Confederate Stamp-Issuing Towns. Alabama: Bridgeville, Greenville, Grove Hill, Livingston, Mobile, Uniontown. Florida: New Smyrna. Georgia: Athens, Macon. Louisiana: Baton Rouge, Mount Lebanon, New Orleans. North Carolina: Hillsboro, Lenoir, Rutherfordton. South Carolina: Charleston, Spartansburg, Unionville. Tennessee: Knoxville, Memphis, Nashville, Rheatown, Tellico Plains, Union City. Texas: Beaumont, Goliad, Gonzales, Hallettsville, Helena, Independence, Port Lavaca, Victoria. Virginia: Danville, Emory, Fredericksburg, Greenwood Depot, Jetersville, Liberty, Lynchburg, Marion, Petersburg, Pittsylvania Court House, Pleasant Shade.

Also see Rarities; U.S. Postmasters' Provisionals.

NEW ORLEANS PROVISIONAL

Connell, Charles. Postmaster general of the Canadian province of New Brunswick before it became part of Canada at Confederation in 1867 and while it was still issuing New Brunswick stamps. Connell used his own picture on the province's 1860 five-cent value (5), but the immediate disapproving uproar caused his dismissal and the stamp was withdrawn before it was issued; it was replaced by one bearing the portrait of Queen Victoria. Although stocks were destroyed, a few copies survived, and today they are rarities.

CONNELL RARITY

Constant Variety. A variety caused by a defect in the printing plate, and hence appearing on every printed impression made by the plate. Typically a constant variety is a single stamp on a sheet and its defect is minor—a minute dot of color or a broken letter, for example. Constant varieties are not separately listed in most catalogs, being of interest only

77

to collectors who hunt for them and specialize in them. There are countless ones in the issues of both the United States and Canada.

Continental Bank Note Company. Printers of the U.S. postage stamps of 1873–75. In 1879 the company merged with the American Bank Note Company, which by then was printing the U.S. stamps.

Also see Bank Note Issues.

CORK PETAL DESIGN

Cork Canceler. A canceling device made by cutting a design on the flat end of a cork, used in early postal days in both the U.S. and Canada as well as in other countries. The carvings were the work of local post-office people, sometimes prosaic and sometimes fanciful; a skull and crossbones, pumpkin face, or valentine heart was a typical favorite design, but many whimsical and comic ones also appeared. Being hand cut, the designs were mostly unfinished in appearance.

Corner Block. A block of usually four stamps from the corner of a pane, with margins on two sides. Corner blocks are collected mainly for the plate numbers or other marginal inscriptions.

Corner Card. The return address and additional matter, if any, appearing in the top left corner of an envelope or postcard. The additional matter normally consists of instructions to the post office in case the piece is undeliverable.

1883 CORNER LETTERS

Corner Letters. Letters appearing in the two lower corners of the early stamps of Great Britain starting with the first stamp in 1840, from which can be determined the stamp's position on the sheet. The left corner letter signified in alphabetical order the horizontal row, and the right corner letter the vertical column. Thus a stamp with A left and B right would be from the first row, the second stamp from the left. Beginning in 1858 the corner letters were placed in the top corners as well, but in opposite order; with only a few exceptions they then appeared on all stamps of Great Britain until the Jubilee issue of 1887, at which time they were discontinued. The arrangement was considered protection against fraud in a seemingly naive theory that it would prevent the piecing together of unpostmarked portions of used stamps to form an apparently unused stamp. Corner letters make reconstruction of an entire sheet—a specialized branch of philately (see Plating)—relatively simple.

Counterfeit. See Forgery.

Counterfoil. A tear-off stub attached to a stamp, intended to be kept by the mailer as a record. Counterfoils have appeared with a few European stamps, but only rarely.

Coupon. A tear-off tab attached to a stamp, carrying a message or graphic device, also called a label. Coupons have appeared with a few European stamps, the best known of which are the Dominical issues of Belgium (see Dominical Label).

Cover. The addressed, stamped, and postmarked part of anything that has gone through the mail. A cover can be a postcard, a self-mailer letter, or a wrapper from a magazine or newspaper or parcel, but in most cases it is simply an envelope. Covers are widely collected, although modern ones seldom attain greater value than the stamps they carry unless they're part of an unusual event; the covers of mail salvaged from an air or sea disaster, for example, can become comparatively valuable if they bear an official notation of the occurrence. Early covers, which often carried multiple post-marks and sometimes stamps from more than one country, can be more valuable than just their stamps would be by themselves. And such philatelic items as bisects (see) cannot be validated unless they're on cover.

Also see First Day Cover.

Crease. A crease in a stamp lessens its value; but many creases, especially if the paper fibers are unbroken, can be removed or rendered invisible (see Renovating Soiled or Damaged Stamps).

cto. Canceled to order (see).

Cut Square. A cutout of a nonadhesive stamp from the envelope or postcard on which it was printed, and cut out in a square regardless of the shape of the stamp. It can also be an imperforate stamp cut from a pane. A cut square with margins is usually more valuable than a cut-to-shape (see).

Cut-to-Shape. As a cut square (see), but cut to follow the shape of the design.

cv, c/v. Catalog value (see).

Cyrillic Alphabet. An alphabet with several modifications widely but not unanimously believed to have been adapted from the ancient Greek by Saint Cyril for the Slavic peoples.

The Cyrillic alphabet generally contains thirty-two characters. It is best recognized by collectors as the one used on stamps of Russia, Bulgaria, Yugoslavia, Serbia, and Montenegro.

Death Masks. Popular name for the five values of the Serbian commemorative issue of 1904 (79–83) marking the centennial of the Karageorgevich dynasty, which had recently returned to power following the assassination of King Alexander V of the Obrenovich family. The stamps are so called because when turned upside down they reveal the assassinated king's likeness. The issue caused a furor because of this, Serbia being part of the Balkans, historically a political hotbed. But despite suspicions and charges, no one ever proved the effect deliberate.

Defect. When a stamp is described as having defects, or being defective, the implication is usually damage of a serious nature. For this reason a stamp with defects is almost always worth only a fraction of its catalog value.

Also see Condition.

Definitive. A stamp of regular issue, as distinguished from a commemorative, special, or special-purpose stamp; generally one of a series of multiple denominations for everyday postal use. Most definitives remain current for extended periods of time, often several years.

United States. In earlier U.S. postal history definitives were replaced or revised more often than they are today. Starting with the first modernized series in 1922, there have been only five definitive issues through the 1970s. The other four are the popular Presidentials of 1938, consisting mostly of the presidents chronologically as far as Coolidge; the Liberty series of 1954, containing some handsome matched portraits of presidents and other notable Americans; the Prominent Americans series of 1965, a gallery of people (some of questionable stature for a long-running definitive issue) and unrelated designs; and the somewhat homely Americana series, which began in 1975.

Canada. The fifty Victorian years of postal service saw several definitive series, and a single one appeared during the comparatively short reign of Edward VII. Then came five George V issues between 1912 and 1935, and four of George VI between 1937 and 1950. The first Elizabeth II series was in 1953; it was followed by a second in 1954, an unattractive one in 1962, one in 1967 unusual for having five collectible varieties of the same six-cent design, one in 1972 showing seven former prime ministers (the first definitives since 1859 to carry likenesses of any persons but the sovereign), and the one started in 1977 featuring colorful, attractive wildflowers on the six low values.

Also see Commemorative; Special Stamp; Special-Purpose Stamps.

Demonetization. The invalidation of a stamp for postal use, done by the issuing authority. This action, if taken at all, is likely to be performed many years after the stamp has been removed from sale. It usually has little effect on catalog value, as the available supplies of the stamp, both mint and used, have stabilized before it is demonetized.

In the United States, the issues up to and including 1862 were demonetized during the Civil War to prevent their use by the Confederacy, and the precanceled Christmas Toys set of 1970 (1415a–1418a) were demonetized early in 1971; no other issues have been demonetized. There have never been any Canadian stamps demonetized, even the oldest provincial issues.

Denomination. The face value of a stamp, the amount of postage it will pay. On stamps used internationally the denomination must appear in arabic numerals, whether or not it also appears in the country's own numerical symbols, if any. This regulation was adopted in 1897 by member countries of the Universal Postal Union (see).
United States. Several U.S. stamps as late as the 1930s appeared without arabic numerals, having instead either Roman numerals or the amount spelled out. They were domestic low values, however, with little international application. But the 1975 Christmas stamps (1579–80) were issued without a denomination showing because a new first-class rate was impending, its inception date unknown when the stamps were being printed; similarly, the three forms of the contingency stamp of 1978 (1735+) bore only the letter A instead of a numeral because they were emergency stamps preprinted to be available any time in case of a postage increase to a suddenly decided new rate. These higher values were not acceptable on overseas mail but were generally honored in Canada.
Canada. Since 1898 there have been no Canadian examples

of stamps without numerals. The then-current definitive series (66–73) lacked them, but was soon changed to include them in the bottom corners of the stamps in place of the previously shown maple leaves.

Departmental Stamp. An official stamp for use only by a particular government department. Nine different U.S. departments had their own stamps in the nineteenth century.

Diadem. The jeweled headdress worn by Queen Victoria on some of her earlier portraits used on stamps of Great Britain and Commonwealth countries. Canada's 1897 Jubilee Issue (50–65) shows both diadem and the later crown in two separate portraits.

Diamond Jubilee. In philately, Queen Victoria's sixtieth anniversary on the throne, in 1897, which in Canada was marked by the country's first commemorative issue. This classic and attractive set comprised sixteen values from half-cent to five dollars (50–65), all of a single design in various colors. It showed two portraits of the queen, one as she looked at her accession in 1837 (this was the old Chalon portrait previously used on Canadian stamps, but for this issue turned right to left), and the other taken from an 1886 painting. The set has always been popular with collectors, and although it contains no true rarities, only a few of the lower values are fairly common.

Also see Chalons; Jubilee.

Die. An original metal engraving of the design for a stamp, from which the printing plates are made. If more than one die is produced, slight but noticeable planned or accidental differences can result, in turn resulting in two or more cataloged varieties of the same stamp.

An example of a die variety occurs in the letter P of the word POSTAGE on both two-cent values (165–166) of the 1930–31 George V issue of Canada. The difference is discernible with a keen naked eye.

Die Proof. A sample printed impression of a stamp made direct from the die (see) during the course of production. Die proofs, although not widely available and theoretically not publicly available at all, are collected as specialties by some philatelists.

Documentary Stamp. A revenue stamp used on business, legal, or official papers.

Dominical Label. A label attached to the stamps of Belgium from 1893 to 1913, instructing against delivery of the letter on Sunday. The label could be detached from the stamp before it was affixed to the envelope, or left in place on the stamp, depending on the sender's views regarding Sunday mail delivery. Absence of the label reduces the catalog value of all the dominical stamps (60–107) by about half.

Double Geneva. Popular name for the 1843 ten-centime stamp (2L1) of the Swiss canton of Geneva. It was a double-size stamp consisting of two identical halves that could be cut apart to form two five-centime stamps. It is an expensive rarity, especially in its uncut ten-centime form.

Also see Rarities: Switzerland Double Geneva.

Drop Letter. A letter for delivery within the same city in which it was mailed.

Ducks, Duck Stamps. Popular names for the U.S. Hunting Permit stamps issued annually since 1934. These are revenue stamps (see), not postage stamps.

Dues. Popular name for postage-due stamps (see).

Edwardian. Categorizes the stamps issued during the reign of King Edward VII by Great Britain, and also to some extent those issued during his reign by the Commonwealth countries.

Effigy. Any likeness representing a person, but in philately usually limited in meaning to a sculpture portrait appearing on a stamp. Effigy stamps, which are common, include such typical ones as the U.S. Washington and Franklin issues of 1908–21.

EFOs. A colloquial term employed in referring collectively to stamp errors, freaks, and oddities. As a general rule its meaning is limited to trivial discrepancies that are curiosities only, and is not intended to include separately cataloged major or minor varieties. Some collectors seek EFOs, most often simply as a diversion.

Also see Error; Freak.

Elizabethan. Categorizes the stamps issued during the reign of Queen Elizabeth II by Great Britain, and also to some extent those issued during her reign by the Commonwealth countries.

Elusive. Occasionally certain common stamps, though neither scarce nor expensive, can be hard to find in the stocks of small dealers or the offerings of private exchange clubs, and hence are described as elusive. Elusiveness develops from time to time in the used higher denominations of even the current issues of a country. Examples of modern common varieties that sometimes become elusive are the U.S. four-and-one-half-cent coil stamp from the 1954 Liberty series (1059) and the Canada reengraved one-dollar value of 1972 (600).

Embossing. Relief printing, in which type or a design is raised on the paper as well as being printed in ink; blind embossing is plain relief, unprinted with ink. Embossing has been used on many nineteenth-century foreign stamps and on the higher values of Great Britain, but it is more common on postal stationery (see), including the envelopes of the United States and Canada.

Emission. Any stamp issue.

Encased Stamps. A stamp enclosed in a transparent holder for use as money during a coin shortage. Encased stamps have usually been a result of a wartime emergency; they were used in the United States during the Civil War, for example, and in Europe during World War I. Being actually more a form of coinage than postal items, encased stamps are generally of greater interest to coin collectors than to stamp collectors.

ENCHASED DESIGN

Enchasement. Any highly elaborate design used to ornament a stamp, as in the rococo 1902–3 definitive issue of the United States (300–313).

Engraving. The cutting of a design in metal, the first step in the production of engraved stamps. The engraving is made by hand on soft steel, line by line, using a hardened-steel pointed tool called a burin. Multiple copies of the engraving are then made by a process invented in the early nineteenth century by Jacob Perkins, who headed the British firm that printed the first line-engraved stamps of Great Britain and a number of British colonies. The Perkins process is a three-step method that allows the original engraved die to reproduce itself as many times as needed to produce the actual printing plates; it goes from hardened original die (design recessed, known also as incised, or intaglio) to transfer roll (design in relief) to printing plate (design recessed).

Also see Printing Methods and How to Distinguish Them.

Entire. A complete cover (see), including stamp, postmark, and address; or a complete unused or used item of postal stationery (see).

Error. A stamp error can be in the design itself, or it can happen during printing. Design errors include artist blunders, anachronisms, wrong pictures or inscriptions, and even simple misspellings. They are commonplace, and watching for new ones is a supplementary hobby for many observant collectors; a few of the more interesting examples are given under the heading Mistakes on Stamps (see). Printing errors include the use of incorrect paper or color; the omission of a color on multicolor stamps; a mistake in perforation size; an engraving flaw; or a missing or inverted section of the design (see Invert). If an error occurs without correction over a stamp's entire printing it is merely a curiosity and does not increase the stamp's value; but if it occurs on only a few of the stamps, as for example has happened several times with inverts, the few stamps can bring extremely high prices. Many of the world's major rarities are printing errors, and some are described under Rarities (see).

Sometimes a stamp is printed upside down on a sheet, or incorrectly printed within a sheet of a different denomination. The upside-down error is called a tete-beche (see), which to prove itself must be collected in the form of at least a pair, unseparated; a few of the scarcest tete-beches are also described under Rarities. The denomination error results in a stamp of wrong color, as when a single five-cent value in the U.S. definitive series of 1916–17 erroneously appeared on sheets of the two-cent value and was hence produced in limited quantity in carmine (467), the color of the two-cent, instead of in its proper five-cent blue (466); the best-known such color error is the Sweden Orange (1a), also described under Rarities.

Essay. A proposed but unaccepted stamp design, usually executed on assignment from a postal authority. Depending on how far a proposal has advanced, an essay can be simply an artist's sketch, or it can be a proof from any later stage of the work.

Europa. The collective name for annual issues produced by various European countries following the central theme of a united Europe and until 1974 with a specific symbol or motif for each year. Sometimes a single stamp design is shared by more than one country. Wheel spokes, tree leaves, and daisy petals are typical of the symbols that have been used, each of them drawn to represent the number of cooperating countries. In 1974 theming was changed to more general topics, allowing the countries broader individual expression; art, ceramics, and landscapes are among the topics that have since been featured.

The Europa issues were introduced in 1956 with six countries participating, a number that reached around twenty in the early 1960s. The issues fell from favor both among issuing countries and collectors after 1961 and 1962, in which years there were incidents of intentional errors, restricted supplies, and other improprieties. By the late 1970s collector interest was largely regained, and the number of participating countries had reached close to thirty.

Also see Omnibus Issue.

Exchange Club. A club organized primarily for the exchange or sale of stamps and other philatelic items among members.

Also see Circuit.

Exhibition. Either a permanent exhibition of an important collection, or a temporary one allied with a philatelic event.

A permanently exhibited collection can be open-ended (with continuing additions and replacements) or closed (no additions or replacements); the latter type is likely to be a well-known collection bequeathed to an institution for public display. The largest open exhibition in the United States is the government display in Washington's Smithsonian Institution, which encompasses a huge worldwide collection. The Smithsonian also houses a major philatelic library.

Permanent exhibitions of private collections are regarded among philatelists with mixed reaction. Their educational and promotional value is unchallenged, but some feel it is outweighed by the fact that they keep many scarce stamps out of circulation forever.

Exhibitions held in connection with a philatelic event consist for the most part of the winning entries in a related competition. So that the ribbon winners in the various categories can be displayed during the event, judging is done before it opens publicly.

Also see Competition Exhibiting.

Expertising. A method of providing educated opinion regarding the authenticity of a stamp or other philatelic item. Expertising is normally performed for a fee by a major stamp society or foundation, where it is done by a committee of philatelic scholars and consultants. The fee is related to the item's catalog value, and in most cases runs somewhere between a few and several dollars. The experts' consensus is rendered on a certificate to which is affixed an identifying photo of the item. It is purely a collective professional opinion and not a guarantee, but is generally considered practically as good as a guarantee.

Expertising is often considered desirable for any stamp of significant value, especially if forgeries of it are known to exist. It may also be required by a prospective buyer of a valuable stamp. To have any item expertised, a service that can be handled by registered mail, consult one of the national philatelic societies for details. Usually it is not necessary to be a member to obtain the service.

Exploded. Describes a stamp booklet with leaves and cover separated from each other and mounted individually on an album page, the usual method of displaying booklets. Another method is to mount the booklet in its original bound state, in which case it is best to surround it with a border of cardboard or other material of its approximate thickness; if it contains interleaves of waxed paper, they should be removed to prevent eventual damage to the stamps.

Face Different. Describes stamps of differing design including color differences. Stamps of the same design but with differences only in paper, watermark, or perforation are not face different. The two one-cent values of the Canada definitive issue of 1912–25 (104–105), while of identical design, are face different because they are of different colors, which is also true of several other values in the issue. The four three-cent values of the U.S. definitive issue of 1922 and later (555, 584, 600, 635), also of identical design, are not face different because their differences are in printing method or perforation, which is also true of several other values in the issue.

Most packets are made up of all face-different stamps, sometimes being so described in dealer price lists. Many collectors, unknowingly or purposely, disregard varieties other than face differences; but where same-face varieties exist, it would be better to exercise care to make sure a supposed expendable duplicate actually is a true duplicate, and not a same-face variety of greater value.

Face, Face Value. The denomination of a stamp, its postal value, as opposed to its catalog value (see).

Facsimile. A likeness of a stamp, sometimes embodying an obvious difference or marking so it cannot be confused with a genuine copy. Unlike forgeries, facsimiles are created without any intent to deceive either collectors or postal patrons; a facsimile of a rarity, for example, is often meant as an artificial filler for an album space that would otherwise remain blank.

Also see Replica.

Fair. A grade of stamp condition. For definitions of recognized grades, see Condition.

Fake. A stamp repaired, altered, or rebuilt to serve a fraudulent purpose, an example being a common stamp modified to pass for an expensive one. Typical faking methods include transforming a used stamp to apparently new condition by cleaning off the cancellation and reapplying gum; altering color by bleaching or other means; adding perforations to imperforate stamps or shearing off existing perforations; changing details in the design; filling in thin spots or sealing up tears; and even creating stamps by joining pieces together. There have been many ingenious and deft repairmen in the history of philately, the work of one nineteenth-century faking expert who was also a collector being so close to undetectable that he is said to have once unwittingly bought one of his own earlier fakes.

Famous Americans. Popular 1940 U.S. issues (859–893) honoring U.S. authors, poets, educators, scientists, composers, artists, and inventors. With five face values in each category, a total of thirty-five Americans both male and female were commemorated. Between 1947 and 1949 five more stamps of identical design were individually issued in a seeming, but not philatelically official, reactivation of the series.

Farley Issues. U.S. special reprintings (752–771) made in 1935 of twenty 1933–34 issues of which postmaster general James A. Farley had presented full sheets, ungummed and in most cases unperforated, to President Roosevelt and other officials. The reprintings were done to make the same unfinished sheets available to collectors, and came about after strong unfavorable opinions were voiced when the presentation sheets started appearing on the market. Each sheet was divided by horizontal and vertical gutters into several panes, the number of panes varying from stamp to stamp; this created many gutter pairs and some gutter blocks, which are priced higher than regular pairs and blocks.

Also see Gutter Pair.

FDC. First day cover (see).

Field. The entire printed area of a stamp. When the printed area continues across the perforations into an adjoining stamp, as in the U.S. 1976 Declaration of Independence issue (1691–1694), it is called a bleed field.

Fine. A grade of stamp condition. For definitions of recognized grades, see Condition.

First Day Cover. A cover postmarked on the first day of issue of the stamp it bears, often carrying a cachet (see) and suitable first day inscription. In the United States and Canada a post office in a place having some connection with the stamp's subject is designated as the first day post office and uses a special postmark with the cancellation line FIRST DAY OF ISSUE; a collector anywhere can send covers for first day handling. Information and instructions on obtaining this service can always be found well in advance in the philatelic press and in the stamp columns of local newspapers.

The term first day cover commonly appears in its abbreviated form, FDC.

First Day Covers as Investments. Although first day covers are widely collected, the modern ones of the United States and Canada, being little more than contrived souvenirs, are unlikely to become any more valuable than the stamps they bear. Unless a first day cover actually goes through the mail, and most do not (often they don't even carry a recipient name and address), it is in effect a canceled-to-order piece, therefore less desirable than a mailed cover; and the first day cancellation date is in most cases fictional, since the post office handles these covers on a mass-production basis over the course of several days or weeks. In addition, many collectors bring or send to the post office quantities of covers for first day cancellation, making it probable that there are more covers in existence than there are collectors for them. For these reasons, modern domestic first day covers should be treated purely as souvenirs, not as an investment opportunity. On the other hand, certain older first day covers, especially coincidental ones—that is, regular mail that just happened to be processed on a stamp's first day of issue—can be highly valuable and have proven to be worthwhile investments.

Also see Canceled to Order.

First Flight Cover. Similar to a first day cover (see) but with evidence relating it to the first flight of a new airmail service instead of the first day of a new stamp's issue. Many first flight covers from airmail's earlier days have attained significant value, having been legitimate pieces of mail in limited number marking an important postal event. There are of course few first flights today.

FIVE AND TEN

Five and Ten. Early nickname for the first two U.S. stamps, the 1847 five- and ten-cent values (1–2). An old story, undocumented and therefore possibly apocryphal, has it that when Frank W. Woolworth opened his first store in Lancaster, Pennsylvania, in 1879, he considered the stamp expression catchy enough to have some bearing on his decision to limit merchandise to five- and ten-cent items.

Flags. Popular name for many sets of stamps showing flags, but mainly taken to mean the U.S. Overrun Countries issues of 1943–44 (909–921). Other U.S. flag sets are the Historic American Flags of 1968 (1345–1354) and the State Flags of 1976 (1633–1682). In Canada a single stamp was issued in 1965 to mark the adoption of the new national flag (439).

Also see State Flags.

Flat Plate. See Printing Methods and How to Distinguish Them.

90

Flaw. A minute transient imperfection on a stamp, caused by a temporary printing fault like a dust speck on a plate. A flaw is a matter of casual interest only, not a catalog minor variety.

Floating Off. A method of removing the paper from stamps vulnerable to water.

Also see Removing Paper from Stamps.

Fluorescence. See Luminescence.

Flyspeck. Colloquial term for a stamp imperfection so slight as to be almost nonexistent. A flyspeck philatelist is one who seeks out such tiny imperfections, and is considered by most collectors to be unjustifiably fussy.

Forgery. A counterfeit of a stamp or postmark intended for a fraudulent purpose. Forged rare stamps, and forged rare postmarks on genuine stamps, are obviously created to defraud collectors and investors. Common stamps have sometimes been forged in volume to defraud postal administrations, a problem that still crops up from time to time; recent U.S. and Canadian examples of this type of forgery are given below. A third kind of postal forgery is the official one carried on by wartime governments, the counterfeiting of enemy stamps to undermine enemy postal systems; this was one of the nuisance weapons of Great Britain during World Wars I and II.

United States. A well-known case occurred in 1949 when over eight million counterfeit three-cent Jeffersons (807) of the 1938 definitive issue were seized; they were considered good enough to pass average scrutiny, and how many of them may actually have been used on mail is not known. Other cases in recent times include forgeries of the 1967 thirteen-cent Kennedy (1287) of the Prominent Americans issue; the 1970 six-cent Eisenhower (1401), of which half a million dollars' worth were confiscated soon after they first appeared; the 1973 ten-cent flags (1509) and Jefferson Memorial (1510) issues, the former of notably poor quality; and the 1975 thirteen-cent Liberty Bell (1595) of the Americana series.

Canada. Recent large-quantity forgeries include the six-cent orange Queen Elizabeth (459) of the 1970 definitive issue and the four-cent Mackenzie King (589) of the 1973 definitive issue. The former was of indifferent quality—poor enough to be readily detected upon examination, but good enough to pass undetected in volume postal handling. This prompted one enterprising individual to buy a large quantity of them to use on return envelopes on a mailing he was sending out. After removing his name and address from all the covers that came back to him postally processed, he sold the covers in the philatelic trade; forged stamps on cover, with a genuine postmark to prove they were actually accepted for postage, are sought by collectors specializing in them and are often more valuable than their legitimate counterparts.

Format. The general form of a stamp, including its size, shape, margins, type style, and graphic look.

Frame. Frame has two philatelic meanings: the outside border of a stamp's design, and the unit used for displaying under glass mounted album pages at a stamp show or competition.

A stamp border frame can be simply a straight line or lines, as in higher values (815–831) of the U.S. Presidential issue of 1938, or elaborate artwork, as in the Pan-American issue of 1901 (294–299). The central illustration or portrait the frame encloses is known as the vignette, and the type matter including denomination and country name is the inscription, the three units together forming the complete stamp design. There are stamp designs without frames, however, examples being the 1973–76 definitive issues of Canada (586–601).

The frame used for displaying mounted album pages at a show usually holds six pages, and shows are often described by the number of frames they comprise; a local club's event might be a twenty-five-frame show, while larger shows might have a hundred or more frames exhibited.

Franchise Stamps. Stamps supplied without cost to various kinds of institutions or semiofficial organizations. Franchise stamps are not regular issues, but separately cataloged types. They have been used in several European countries.

Franking. A privilege extended to officials in many countries, whereby the official's written or printed initials or signature in place of the stamp is accepted as payment of postage. In the United States and Canada the franking privilege is accorded to members of legislative bodies and certain other authorities for specified kinds of mail.

ELABORATE FRAME DESIGN

Freak. A stamp with something abnormal about it, the stamp being the only one of its kind or one of very few. A freak is a matter of casual interest, but not a catalog minor variety.

Front. The part of a cover (see) containing address and postmarked stamps, usually called a front only when it is detached from the cover. In the case of an envelope, for instance, it is the single rectangle of front paper that is left when the sealing flap and the back are cut away. Early covers were sometimes cut to front, and are usually less valuable for it; today's practice is to leave the entire cover intact.

Fugitive Ink. Nonfixed ink, usually one that is soluble in water or other fluids, used in printing stamps and post-marking. Fugitive inks are not widely used on stamps today, but during the nineteenth century they were common as preventives against stamp cleaning for reuse. Their appearance in postmarks is also limited today, and has mostly been for the purpose of adding color to the mark; purple, red, and other postmark colors should be considered fugitive in working with the stamps. Stamps with fugitive inks must be specially treated when removing paper from them.

Also see Removing Paper from Stamps.

Georgian. Categorizes the stamps issued during the reigns of King George V and King George VI by Great Britain, and also to some extent those issued during their reigns by the Commonwealth countries.

GERMANIA

Germania. The familiar classic female profile that appeared on the definitive stamps of Germany from 1900 to 1921. The design symbolized the German Empire, and was adapted from a portrait of a Wagnerian opera singer.

German Occupation Issues. German stamps overprinted for use in occupied countries in the two world wars. In World War I German issues were imposed on Belgium, Poland, Romania, and the Baltic states of Estonia, Latvia, and Lithuania. In World War II the affected countries were Poland and the Baltics again, as well as Luxembourg and the Ukraine.

German States. The separate kingdoms, grand duchies, principalities, and city-states totaling about fifteen in number that federated in 1871 to form the German Empire. Before federation most issued their own stamps, all of which were superseded by stamps of Germany beginning in 1872.

Gibbons, Stanley. One of the world's earliest stamp dealers, who started in business in Plymouth, England, in 1856. The Gibbons catalog, which began in 1865 as a sixteen-page booklet and now comes in several editions, is the one most widely used in British Commonwealth countries except Canada.

Glassine. A thin but tough translucent paper. In philately the term is accepted to mean the glassine envelopes that are used both by dealers and collectors for packaging and storing stamps.

Glassine envelopes come in several numbered sizes, which are often referred to simply by number. Numbers with sizes in inches follow:

1	$1\frac{3}{4} \times 2\frac{7}{8}$	6	$3\frac{3}{4} \times 6\frac{3}{4}$
$1\frac{1}{2}$	$2\frac{1}{16} \times 3\frac{1}{2}$	7	$4\frac{1}{8} \times 6\frac{1}{4}$
2	$2\frac{5}{16} \times 3\frac{5}{8}$	8	$4\frac{1}{2} \times 6\frac{5}{8}$
3	$2\frac{1}{2} \times 4\frac{1}{4}$	9	$4 \times 8\frac{7}{8}$
4	$3\frac{1}{4} \times 4\frac{7}{8}$	10	$4\frac{1}{8} \times 9\frac{1}{2}$
$4\frac{1}{2}$	$3\frac{1}{8} \times 5\frac{1}{16}$	11	$4\frac{1}{2} \times 10\frac{3}{8}$
5	$3\frac{1}{2} \times 6$		

Good. A grade of stamp condition. For definitions of recognized grades, see Condition.

Government Imitations. Official imitations of stamps made by the issuing authority after the original plates have been destroyed, or reprints made from plates still in existence after a stamp has been demonetized. Government imitations in quantity are infrequent today; when produced in former times they were usually for the purpose of increasing a stamp's floating stock for collectors. The practice is considered unethical by most collectors.

Also see Demonetization.

Granite Paper. See Paper Types and How to Distinguish Them.

Grangerizing. A method of creating fake stamps by fitting together pieces cut selectively from genuine stamps. Grangerizing was commonly done by some of the most expert of the nineteenth-century counterfeiters. The term derives from James Granger, a writer whose eighteenth-century history book was illustrated with pictures cut from various sources.

Graphite. Lines of graphite were printed on the backs of some stamps of Great Britain starting in 1957 during the first experiments with electronic letter-facing machines used in automatic canceling. In 1959 the graphite lines were superseded by phosphor bands on the front of the stamps.

Also see Tagged.

Grease Stains on Stamps. See Renovating Soiled or Damaged Stamps.

Grill. A geometric pattern made with tiny squares cut into the fibers of stamp paper. Grills were used in several series of U.S. stamps between 1867 and 1871. The purpose of the grill was to prevent removal of the cancellation for reuse of the stamp; the canceling ink would be absorbed into the broken fibers and become ineradicable. A similar arrangement was used on the stamps of Peru for a short time a few years later.

There were several types of U.S. grills; one type known as a Z-grill appeared on three of the country's rarest stamps including the 1867 one-cent Franklin (85a), of which only two copies are known.

The term grill also applies to the feint-ruled squares that appear on some unprinted album pages to assist in the straight and symmetrical placement of stamps.

Also see Rarities; U.S. Franklin Z-Grill.

Guide Line. Guide lines appear on full press sheets of stamps for purposes mostly in connection with the alignment or registration of printing, perforating, and cutting. They are placed outside the live printed area and thus do not show on the stamps, but some can usually be seen on the margins of panes. Another kind of guide line that is important philatelically is caused by a printing-plate join and appears at regular intervals between stamps on the rolls of many U.S. and Canadian coil varieties; two coil stamps with a line showing between them are commonly collected as a line pair.

Also see Coil Stamps; Line Pair; Pane.

Guillotine Perforation. See Perforation.

Gum. The condition of the gum on unused stamps is an important factor in evaluating them. Current practice is to discount modern issues carrying anything other than perfect gum, which understandably is less common on earlier stamps. Since even light or spot hinging marks the gum, and heavy hinging disturbs and often removes a portion of it, meticulous mint collectors today don't hinge stamps at all. Unhinged stamps are described in price lists and sale catalogs as never hinged (*nh*), a condition now the expected standard for new issues.

Some collectors consider preoccupation with *nh* condition to be a fetish, arguing that slight gum marking in no way alters the stamp's appearance and should have no effect on its value; they feel that methods other than hinging add unnecessary bulk to album pages, obscure some of a stamp's beauty, and sometimes in their own way eventually harm a stamp more than hinging may. Their arguments appear valid, and it does seem that the general collector might well leave insistence on *nh* condition to the purists and as a bonus save money on his purchases, even though the stamps will probably also realize less when they are sold.

In a different category is original gum (*og*), a description found most often in reference to earlier stamps. It is common for unused early stamps to have lost their gum for any of several reasons, including being stuck down on an album page. Regumming a gumless unused stamp has always been a favorite trick of faking experts, although most such efforts can usually be detected by an expert's scrutiny. But true original gum is for some older issues a legitimate reason for a premium price.

Gutter. On full press sheets of stamps, the space left between the individual panes. This space becomes the paper margin around the stamps and outside the perforations when the press sheets are cut into panes. The irritating straight edges found on many earlier U.S. stamps were caused by lack of a gutter on the press sheets, which when quartered left straight edges on two full sides of each pane, for a total of nineteen straight-edge stamps on every one-hundred-stamp pane. It wasn't until well into the 1930s, largely as a result of collector complaints, that gutters were made universal in U.S. printings.

Gutter Pair. Any pair of stamps separated horizontally or vertically by a gutter (see) instead of being normally adjacent. Gutter pairs have appeared on the commemorative stamps of Great Britain since the 1972 Silver Wedding issue (683–684), and on the stamps of a few other countries including the United States, where they are found on some of the 1933–34

BRITISH GUTTER PAIR

Farley issues (see). They are widely collected, especially in Great Britain.

Hairline. Describes a fine-line printing defect on a stamp, caused by a minute scratch or similar flaw on the printing plate. A hairline defect can take the form of an unwanted print line, or conversely, a line scratched from the printed area.

Handback. A cover hand-canceled at the post office window and handed back to the customer instead of being routed through the mail channels. Handbacks are procured by collectors usually for the purpose of obtaining special commemorative cancellations, or sometimes simply to be sure of getting a carefully placed cancellation.

Also see First Day Cover.

Handstamp. A postal cancellation applied by hand, instead of by canceling machine; also, the rubber stamp with which the cancellation is applied. Generally, stamping by hand is done today only for philatelic purposes or on parcels and similar items that don't lend themselves to automatic handling.

Before adhesive stamps appeared, payment of postage was recorded on the envelope by a handstamp, which was commonly referred to simply as a stamp, a term that endured to become the name for the new adhesives.

Harris. A regularly issued catalog of the stamps of the United States, Canada, and the United Nations, published by H. E. Harris & Co. of Boston. It is the firm's actual price list and is widely used as a general price reference for the stamps it covers.

Harrow Perforation. See Perforation.

Harvesters. Popular name for almost one hundred stamps of Hungary issued between 1916 and 1924 and bearing an illustration of two workers harvesting wheat.

Hatching. The multiple thin close lines, either parallel or crossed, that appear for decorative or shading effects in engraving and sometimes other types of printing; also called crosshatching.

Hatching appeared commonly on earlier stamps, but is used much less today. Examples of hatching with details visible to the naked eye are on the three U.S. three-cent

HATCHED DESIGN

97

Washington issues of 1861–62 (64–66) and the several other issues of the same design; and on the Canada one-cent Queen Victoria of 1859 (14).

Hawaiian Missionaries. Popular name for the first four stamps of Hawaii (1–4) issued in 1851, so called because they are believed to have been used mostly on mail sent home by American missionaries in the islands. They are among the world's most valuable rarities.

Also see Rarities: Hawaiian Missionaries.

Health Stamps. Semipostal stamps on which the surtax is used to help support institutions or activities devoted to promoting health or fitness. The best-known health stamps are those of New Zealand, which have been issued annually since 1929; their surtax has almost invariably gone toward the maintenance of children's health camps.

Also see Semipostal.

Heliogravure. See Printing Methods and How to Distinguish Them.

Hidalgos. Popular name for over 125 early stamps of Mexico that bore a portrait of Miguel Hidalgo y Costilla, 1753–1811, a parish priest and revolutionary, considered the father of Mexican independence. Hidalgo appeared on the first Mexican stamp in 1856 and on most others until 1885, and then on two more in 1892.

Hill, Sir Rowland (1795–1879). British government official, generally credited with being the originator of the postage stamp. While attached to the British Treasury Department he early in 1840 instituted a standard rate of one penny for all domestic mail regardless of distance, and in May of that year introduced the first adhesive postage stamp, the Penny Black (see).

Hinge. See Mounting Methods.

Hingeless Album. See Album.

Humidifier, Humidor. A device for removing paper from stamps, or separating stuck-together stamps, without soaking. It is a small airtight container in which the stamps to be treated are placed along with a wettable pad for moistening the sealed-in air. The treatment usually loosens adhesion fairly fast; depending on the type of gum used, fifteen or twenty minutes are often ample.

Also see Removing Paper from Stamps.

Imperforate. Describes stamps without perforations, generally the earliest stamps. Perforated stamps were introduced in Great Britain in 1854, and within a few years they became the standard in most stamp-issuing countries.

Before perforations, stamps had to be cut from the sheet with scissors or knife. This led to uneven margins, or complete cutoff of a margin and even part of the design; as a result, well-centered imperforates with generous margins command a premium price.

Also see Perforation.

Impression. Broadly, any printed copy of anything; in philately the term is generally limited to meaning a proof copy of the stamp's actual design taken from a die or printing plate at some stage of production.

Indicia. A permit or other marking valid as payment for postage appearing on an envelope or card in place of a stamp on bulk or government mail. The term indicia is the plural of indicium, but it is used colloquially as a singular noun.

Inscription. The portion of a stamp design containing the type matter, including denomination and country name. The complete design consists of frame (the outside border), vignette (the portrait or illustration), and inscription, although the frame is often omitted on today's stamps. There have been U.S. stamps with incomplete inscriptions; no country name appeared on the Pilgrim Tercentenary issue of 1920 (548–550), for example, and no denomination on the Christmas issue of 1975 (1579–1580) and the A stamp of 1978 (1735+).

Also see Denomination.

Insuring a Stamp Collection. Standard homeowner's insurance policies limit the coverage on philatelic material to a few hundred dollars, an amount probably sufficient for the vast numbers of hobbyist collectors whose albums hold few if any stamps besides common varieties. But for advanced collectors and specialists, investors, and philatelic scholars, homeowner's coverage is clearly inadequate and must be supplemented by either a floater endorsement at added premium or a completely separate policy.

A separate policy that takes into consideration the special nature of philatelic material is usually the best choice. It should offer specifically listed coverages against loss wherever any part of the collection may happen to be: at home, in a bank safety deposit box, on exhibition, or in transit by mail, public carrier, or private automobile. It should also offer automatic coverage of newly acquired items right from their date of acquisition, and possibly, because of inflation, automatic percentage increases in total coverage periodically. Check the policy's provisions concerning these details when shopping for collection insurance.

Proof-of-loss requirements differ from company to company and should also be considered in evaluating available policies. Some companies require more detailed inventorying than others, including the listing of greater numbers of individual items. In addition, some companies offer premium discounts for collections recorded on microfilm, or for collections of which a specified percentage of inventory value is kept in a safety deposit box.

Major national philatelic societies offer insurance to members that is often more suited to collector needs and lower in cost than policies available on the open market. It can sometimes be worthwhile to join one of these organizations purely to be eligible for its insurance plan; but as with any serious purchase, it's always sensible to compare the plan before buying. In any case, some sort of insurance in addition to the standard homeowner's policy should be obtained for any collection that will realize much more than a few hundred dollars from its sale.

Also see Inventorying a Stamp Collection; Protecting Stamp Collections from Theft.

Intaglio. See Printing Methods and How to Distinguish Them.

Interrupted Perforation. A method of perforating that omits one or a few holes from the perforated row, its objective being to retain some of the strength of the unbroken paper; also known as syncopated perforation. It was used experimentally on early coil stamps of the United States, and has also appeared on stamps of Peru and the Netherlands.

Also see Perforation.

Invalidation. See Demonetization.

Inventorying a Stamp Collection. In setting up and maintaining a philatelic inventory system, keep in mind that while the inventory can be useful in tax or estate matters (paragraph 6 below), its main purpose is to document your claim in the event of any insured loss. As long as it is adequate for this it needn't list every stamp in the collection individually, especially every common one. And because of the fluid nature of most stamp holdings—frequent acquisitions and sometimes selloffs—the system should be as simple as possible so that keeping the inventory updated won't become burdensome.

The information given in the inventory will vary according to the type and value of the material. The following suggestions are meant only as starters; adapt from them to set up the system that works best for you and your collection.

1. General collections worth no more than a few hundred dollars (those that are adequately covered by the usual five-hundred-dollar philatelic limit in a standard homeowner's insurance policy) can often be sufficiently described by listing the countries represented along with the number of stamps, and whether new or used, of each, and also the approximated total catalog value of the collection. But remember that since replacement cost for common material is usually well below catalog value, any general collection consisting mostly of common stamps—what the dealer trade calls packet material—will bring only a fraction of catalog value from sale or insurance settlement (a professional largely ignores packet material in appraising collections).

2. Details noting expensive items or blanket completeness can be added in simple manner. Examples: "U.S. includes mint singles of all 1929 Kansas and Nebraska overprints." "Canada used singles complete 246 through 699 except 302." Consolidation of consecutive numbers is not necessarily understood to include minor varieties, which if somewhat valuable should be listed separately.

3. In general, anything in a collection that is less than common—say anything worth more than a very few dollars—should be separately noted. Thus the more valuable a collection is, the more detailed the inventory should be to afford the best documentation in case of loss.

4. Condition should always be noted, since it directly affects value; particulars of any defects should be accurately described, as should any superior features commanding a premium.

5. Blocks, line pairs, covers, and similar miscellaneous material need not be listed separately unless they're of particular value. In the case of covers that are of value mainly because of their postal markings, the markings should be noted; better, the covers should be machine-copied.

6. Acquisition costs for individually listed items should be given, and original bills of sale retained to support them; this information will give the inventory validity for tax and estate purposes. Expertising documents should be kept as part of the inventory, as they may also be required by an appraiser. (If confidentiality is desired, indicate costs in a simple letter code. Privately adopt any word or phrase of ten letters in which no letter appears more than once, so each letter in order can represent a digit from 1 through 0. Thus if the code word were *DISPATCHER*, *IR* would mean 20 and *DHA* would mean 185.)

Other ways to maintain an inventory include catalog checkoff and microfilming. Checking off owned numbers in a catalog is a method that allows easy continuous updating for single stamp varieties, but requires periodic transfer of check marks to new updated catalogs as well as the addition of such further information as notes on condition and listings of miscellaneous material. Another drawback to this method is that it may not be practical to keep catalogs and collection at different locations, but in case of fire inventory and stamps should not be under the same roof.

Microfilming of album pages can be done commercially in just about any city; companies offering the service appear in the classified section of the telephone directory. This system, which also requires supporting notes, is most practical for static parts of a collection with minimum turnover in the material. For those who compete in shows microfilming is also a useful means of forming a permanent record of the exhibit pages, which because of their travels are more vulnerable to loss than albums that are housed in one place. Although not costly in relation to valuable philatelic property, microfilming is usually not worthwhile for common stamps (for additional on microfilming, see Protecting Stamp Collections from Theft, paragraph 6).

Also see Catalog Value; Insuring a Stamp Collection.

Invert. A stamp with any part of the design appearing upside down because of a printing mistake, as when partially printed sheets are fed back to the press in the wrong direction for a second or other additional color. Occasionally a portion of a design has appeared upside down right on the printing plate—an example is the inverted figure 5 on an 1874 Egyptian issue (26)—but the resultant stamp is not an invert; it is simply a design error, of possible interest but adding no particular value to the stamp. There are also instances of a complete stamp appearing upside down on the sheet, and these are not inverts either, but rather tete-beches.

There are several inverts, mostly U.S. issues, among the well-known stamp rarities. One U.S. invert that wasn't allowed to become a rarity, however, was the 1962 Dag Hammarskjold commemorative, a few sheets of which were discovered with the color background upside down; when they came to light millions more were printed like them, resulting in two major catalog varieties (1203–1204) of the same stamp—a USPS action that caused outcry, both pro and con, from collectors.

Also see Error; Rarities: Japanese Invert, U.S. Inverts, India Queen Victoria Invert; Tete-Beche.

Iron Curtain Countries. Generally speaking the stamps of countries within the Soviet Union's sphere of influence are not considered desirable by collectors. A main reason for their unpopularity is the multitude of postally unneeded emissions that come out of many Iron Curtain countries. A single example is Russia itself, which has been averaging over one hundred varieties a year for several years and now has three or four times as many cataloged numbers as the United States in regular stamps alone, and perhaps seven or eight times as many as Canada; the comparative figures are approximate because they are constantly changing.

Iron Curtain stamps are mostly not sold originally through the philatelic trade at all, but direct by state agencies, usually for a premium above face value for mint copies and a discount from face for copies canceled to order to simulate used condition. Most are produced for collectors, and would probably not be available in the countries' post offices or used on their domestic or international mail. To be sure of validity if you want an Iron Curtain representation in your collection, include only used varieties that have passed through international mails. The Iron Curtain stigma applies to only the modern era, and does not include Imperial Russia before the revolution, Communist Russia in

U.S. FAMOUS AIRMAIL INVERT

103

its early days, or the other Iron Curtain countries before they fell under Russian influence.

Japanese Occupation Issues. Stamps issued by several southeast Asian countries while they were under Japanese occupation during World War II. Countries included Brunei, Burma, Dutch East Indies, Hong Kong, Malaysia, North Borneo, Philippines, and Sarawak. In some cases the issues were the country's own stamps with Japanese overprint, in others they were specially designed occupation stamps.

Jubilee. In philately the term usually refers to a major anniversary of the accession of a British sovereign, an event marked by commemorative issues in most British Commonwealth countries. The 1887 multidenomination Golden Jubilee issue of Great Britain (111–122) commemorated the fiftieth anniversary of Queen Victoria's accession, and then remained in use throughout the balance of her reign, which lasted another fourteen years. Britain has subsequently issued Silver Jubilee stamps marking the twenty-fifth anniversaries of George V in 1935 (226–229) and Elizabeth II in 1977 (810–814).

Canada's first commemorative issue for any purpose was the long 1897 set (50–65) marking Queen Victoria's Diamond Jubilee, her sixtieth anniversary. George V's Silver Jubilee was commemorated with a six-stamp set (211–216) and Elizabeth II's with a single stamp (704).

In early 1977 a group of twenty-four small British Commonwealth countries joined together to release an unusual omnibus series marking Elizabeth's Silver Jubilee. Each country issued three stamps, all of which had certain common format characteristics. The most interesting feature of the series was a coordinated picture story of the queen's coronation in 1953; one stamp from each country illustrated an event of coronation day. The twenty-four events ran in sequence by country alphabetically, starting with Ascension showing the queen leaving Buckingham Palace for the ceremony and ending with Turks and Caicos Islands showing the royal family on the palace balcony after the ceremony's conclusion.

Also see Diamond Jubilee; Omnibus Issue.

Kangaroos. Popular name for over fifty stamps of Australia showing a kangaroo against a map outline of the country. The design appeared in 1913 on the country's entire first

AUSTRALIA KANGAROO ISSUE

issue (1–15), and reappeared many times thereafter until as late as 1945.

Kansas and Nebraska Issues. In 1929 the United States overprinted the one-cent to ten-cent values of the 1922 regular issue with *Kans.* (658–668) or *Nebr.* (669–679) for sale in the two states everywhere but in a few cities. The overprints were produced in an attempt to stop burglary losses that had been occurring at post offices in the states, but the issues were discontinued after the initial printings were exhausted in about a year. One or two of the values are fairly common today, but most have at least some degree of scarcity. Such issues, neither definitive nor commemorative, are known as special issues.

NEBRASKA OVERPRINT

Kennedys. Popular name for the hundreds of stamps that were issued all over the world to commemorate President John F. Kennedy after his assassination in 1963. Over seventy countries contributed to this outpouring, many of them obviously seeking to capitalize on the thousands of new collectors of Kennedy memorabilia. For this reason, and because few of the issues filled a postal need, most of the stamps are generally rated of little philatelic value.

Key Type. A stamp design used by mother countries as a common pattern for stamps of smaller dependencies, usually showing everything but the colony name and the currency denomination, which are inserted by a second plate when the stamps are being printed. Key-type stamps have been widely used for dependencies of France, Germany, Great Britain, Portugal, and Spain.

Killer. The part of the cancellation that hits on the stamp, defacing it against further postal use.

Also see Cancellation.

Kiloware. A mixture package of used foreign stamps of a single country presumably packed and sealed in the country of origin, usually by the kilogram or other metric weight, or sometimes by the pound. Some collectors consider kiloware to offer cleaner stamps and better unpicked value potential than regular mixtures, which may not be invariably true.

Also see Mixture.

Kiss Stamp. On some booklet panes of Great Britain one space shows a large *X* instead of a postage stamp, the *X* space being popularly known as a kiss stamp.

Also see Booklet.

Label. Loosely, any adhesive sticker used on a cover except an actual postage stamp. Christmas and other health or charity seals are examples of labels in this broad sense, as are the routing stickers employed by the USPS on sorted or rough-sorted mail bundles.

Strictly, label means a tear-off tab attached to a stamp and carrying a message or graphic device. Labels have been used with certain European stamps, the best-known examples being the 1893–1913 Dominical issues of Belgium.

Also see Dominical Label; Routing Stickers.

Laid Paper. See Paper Types and How to Distinguish Them.

Lake. A deep red color often used on stamps, and because of its name a common cause of confusion among beginning collectors, who might naturally expect it to be a green or blue water shade.

LARGE QUEEN

Large Queens. Popular name for the 1868 Queen Victoria issue of Canada (21–33), consisting of eight values from half-cent to fifteen cents, all bearing a profile portrait of the queen. The half-cent value, being somewhat smaller than the others, is sometimes erroneously considered a Small Queen. The Small Queens, however, were separate issues; they replaced the Large Queens in 1870. None of the Large Queens are common, with most values and minor varieties being at least scarce unused. One two-cent denomination (32), is Canada's most expensive rarity.

Also see Rarities: Canada Large Queens; Small Queens.

Latins. Popular name for the stamps of France, Italy, Portugal, and Spain collectively. The term is also applied occasionally to the stamps of Latin America.

Laying Out Attractive Album Pages. In arranging stamps on plain or quadrilled unprinted album pages there are two objectives to strive for: The arrangement should be pleasing, and it should afford proper exposition of what you're attempting to feature. A few layout suggestions follow.

1. Do not crowd the page. Twenty or so small stamps are usually enough to fill a standard page attractively. With bigger stamps allow fewer, the number depending on their size and shape.

2. A page shouldn't look sparse by having too few stamps, but there are many reasonable exceptions to this, usually for the purpose of highlighting a stamp or group of stamps. Thus a page could quite properly contain only a

short set, or even one single stamp, but for effectiveness this arrangement should be used only sparingly and only for stamps that offer special interest.

3. As far as possible a page should be laid out with a balanced look, but this doesn't mean that all pages must be completely symmetrical, which overall could give a characterless appearance. Plan every layout by first moving the stamps around on the page until an effective, pleasing look is achieved. Catalog numerical order or order of monetary value should often be disregarded, especially for sets with stamps of differing shapes or sizes. Examples of such are the U.S. National Parks issue of 1934 (740–749) and the Canada Silver Jubilee issue of 1946 (211–216), neither of which is in numerical or face-value order when arranged for visual balance.

4. Allow sufficient space for any writeups or other material that will also appear on the page. Will there be a single writeup for the entire page, or one for each stamp or set? It is best if the writeups are done at this stage, so the amount of space they will need is known.

5. A ruled box around each stamp is optional but preferable, as it defines the stamp and keeps it from appearing to float on the page. Ruling can be done with a fine black pen or for special effect with a colored pencil, which should be kept freshly pointed. For a multistamp page make the box between $\frac{1}{8}$ and $\frac{1}{16}$ of an inch bigger than the stamp in both directions; make the boxes somewhat larger than that for pages designed to contain only a few featured stamps, and if desired, big enough to also hold a writeup. Experiment to find the best size relationship for each page.

Quadrille pages simplify box ruling, which can also be simplified for completely plain pages by the use of a philatelic template or transparent grid, both available from many stamp dealers. Templates have cutouts for all stamp sizes; to avoid line smearing when working with ink, use them only for marking the corner points of the box. Do this lightly with a sharp pencil, then proceed with a ruler. Grids require the use of a light table, which is basically a sheet of frosted glass with a strong light beneath and can easily be improvised; the grid is placed on the glass with the album page over it so the grid lines show through to act as ruling guides.

Examples of bad or uninteresting page layouts *(left)*, **with improvements** *(right)*

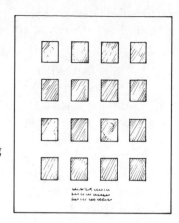

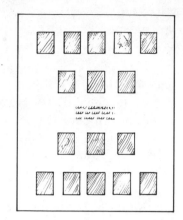

Example 1
Left: Sixteen regular-size stamps in an arrangement symmetrical but lacking interest. Right: Still symmetrical, but in more interesting and attractive layout.

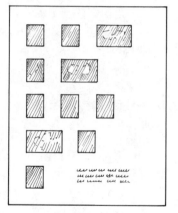

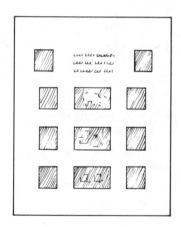

Example 2
Left: Eight regular-size stamps with three horizontal commemoratives, arranged without visual organization (but possibly in order of denominational values, which in mixed sets like this should be disregarded). Right: Now in attractive arrangement that loses nothing if denominations are out of order.

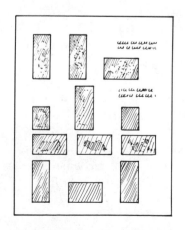

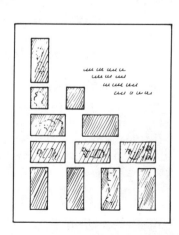

Example 3
Left: Two regular-size stamps with five horizontal and five vertical commemoratives, in completely unorganized and unattractive layout. Right: A demonstration of how such a combination of various shapes can be given an organized look, and how a page layout need not be symmetrical to be at least reasonably attractive.

6. As a general rule in collections by country, sets should be kept together and issuance years should be in order and properly grouped, suggestions that of course do not apply to topical collections.

Since one of the reasons for using an unprinted album is to give your collection a personal flavor, the above are guidelines rather than rules, as are the illustrated examples. Set tasteful organization and effective display as your goals, and your pages will please both you and your collection's viewers.

Also see Collateral; Competition Exhibiting; Writeups and How to Prepare Them.

League of Nations Stamps. Regular stamps of Switzerland overprinted in various styles for use by the League of Nations at its headquarters in Geneva. The league was formed in 1919 and dissolved in 1946, and the overprints were in use from 1922 until its dissolution. They are classed as Switzerland official stamps (2O1–2O90).

SWITZERLAND LEAGUE OF NATIONS OVERPRINT

Letterpress. See Printing Methods and How to Distinguish Them.

Liberty Issue. U.S. definitive issue (1030–1059a) introduced in 1954 and gradually superseded by the Prominent Americans issue starting in 1965. The Liberty series eventually contained twenty-seven values up to five dollars. It showed several American historical landmarks as well as portraits of U.S. presidents and other notable Americans. There are sixteen such portraits in the series, all of matching simple design except for the eight-cent Pershing stamp; together they make up what is considered by many collectors to be the most handsome portrait series of all U.S. definitive issues.

LIBERTY PORTRAIT

Line Engraving. Another name for engraving (see).

Line Pair. A pair of coil stamps on which a printed line appears beside or on the row of perforations between them. The line is caused by the join in the printing plate, and usually appears between every twenty-fourth or twenty-fifth stamp on the coil. Line pairs are found on the stamps of the United States and Canada, and are widely collected specialties.

COIL LINE PAIR

Also see Coil Stamps.

Line Perforation. See Perforation.

Lithography. See Printing Methods and How to Distinguish Them.

Locals. Stamps issued officially or by private postal services valid only within specified local areas. In the United States locals were issued by private firms starting in 1844 and continuing until 1861 when the government took over all mail services. Over six hundred U.S. local stamps, most of them scarce or rare, are recognized by catalogs. They were issued in many cities and towns throughout the country by a total of around one hundred fifty firms. Since there were no exclusive area franchises, the major cities each had several issuing companies, although none approached the number in New York, where there were about fifty. There are no Canada locals with general catalog recognition.

Also see Carriers' Stamps.

London-to-London Flight Stamp. In September 1927 a two-man plane set out from London, Ontario, in an attempt to fly to London, England; it disappeared over the Atlantic after taking off from Saint John's, Newfoundland. Under government supervision one hundred copies of a special twenty-five-cent stamp were printed to be used on the limited mail the flight was authorized to carry. The stamp bore the inscription LONDON TO LONDON and the pictures of the pilot and navigator. All except two or three copies were on the mail that went down with the plane, and these few exist today, as well as a single cover that was mistakenly left behind when the flight started out for the second time (a start three days earlier had been aborted and the plane with its canceled mail had returned home). Not being an official government issue, the London-to-London stamp is not listed by most catalogs.

Luminescence. A fluorescent or phosphorescent emission of light occurring when a surface is exposed to ultraviolet rays. Fluorescence occurs only while the surface is being exposed to the ultraviolet; phosphorescence additionally emits afterglow. Luminescent properties are applied to stamps to allow post office use of electronic mail-processing machines. Stamps so treated are called tagged.

Also see Tagging.

Lyman's. A catalog of Canada and British North America stamps, issued annually in Toronto and widely used by

Canadian collectors and dealers.

Also see Catalog.

M, m. Mint (see).

Magenta. Popular name for the world's most valuable stamp, the British Guiana one-cent issue of 1856 (13), of which only one copy is known to exist.

See Rarities: British Guiana Magenta.

Magnifier. A magnifying glass is one of stamp collecting's few indispensable accessories, and choosing the right glass for your needs requires only an understanding of two or three simple facts. Magnifying power is expressed by number, the number representing the optical increase in the size of an object compared with its actual size when viewed without a glass from the normal ten inches away. Thus with a five-power (expressed 5x) magnifier, the object appears to be five times actual size. Because of a basic principle of optics, a magnifier's field of vision decreases in area as its power increases; the higher the power, the smaller the field. For this reason it is helpful to have two magnifiers, a low-power one for viewing the whole stamp and a 5x or 6x one for close examination of details. A magnifier costing only two or three dollars is usually adequate for anyone but the serious specialist or philatelic scholar; higher cost basically brings increased distortion-free quality in the glass, not really a major need for the average collector. Many types of magnifiers are commonly available, including lighted and folding pocket models. An advantage of the latter is that they can be conveniently carried along for use when visiting shows, bourses, and dealers' stores.

Mail Auction. See Auction.

Map Stamps. Maps have long been frequently used and popularly accepted in stamp designs. Through the late 1970s they have appeared only on commemoratives in the United States (nine times) and Canada (four times), but in several countries—Australia is one example—they have enjoyed longtime usage on definitive issues. The world's first map stamp was Canada's 1898 two-cent Imperial Penny Postage issue (85–86), often considered to be also the first Christmas stamp because of its inscription XMAS 1898. The first stamps of Latvia (1–2) issued in 1918 shortly following

World War I had nonrelevant map sections on the reverse, as they were printed on the backs of German military maps. On at least two occasions stamp maps incorrectly drawn have been the cause of international repercussions (see Mistakes on Stamps: Argentina, Dominican Republic, Nicaragua).

Margin. In philately margin means the outside edges of full stamp sheets or booklet panes, or the outside edges of individual stamps. The margins on individual stamps are significant because they're the determinants of the stamp's centering, an important factor in assessing value.

Stamp margins are of particular concern on early imperforate issues, especially issues in which the identical stamps were also produced perforated. In the early days stamps were simply cut from sheets with scissors; since little or no care was exercised, many imperforates had part of the design cut into, with the result that fully margined and reasonably centered copies are usually at a premium. A greater problem, however, was the fakery that often occurred on stamps issued both unperforated and perforated; when the former were more valuable than the latter it was a common trick to simply cut off the perforations, creating an imperforate copy for the unwary. For this reason any of these early imperforates should be treated with suspicion if the margins are tiny or missing; actually, for any imperforate, the wider the margins on all sides, the higher the stamp's value. Pairs and blocks of imperforate stamps demonstrate genuineness and are sought by many collectors, but for most early stamps they are nonexistent, rare, or scarce.

Marianne. The name given to portraits of a female head symbolizing France and appearing on over forty French definitive issues of 1944–47.

Maximum Card. An oversize card created as a postal souvenir, usually in connection with a commemorative stamp issue, and bearing certain fairly standard features: It generally carries an allover picture relating to the stamp, and the stamp is affixed directly onto the picture and tied to the card with a first day or other pertinent postmark. Sometimes a white space is left for an address, but not always, since the card is seldom intended for mail use. Commercially printed cards are available for most new commemorative issues, and in addition many collectors of them make their own cards by mounting relevant pictures on cardboard. Collecting these artificial mementos is a specialization of little or no interest to the average stamp collector.

Medallion. An element commonly used in stamp design and consisting of a portrait or other illustration set in a round or oval frame. Many stamp series are popularly referred to as medallions, particularly the 1850–65 Leopold I definitives of Belgium (3–16).

Merry Widow. Early popular name for the U.S. ten-cent special-delivery stamp of 1908 (E7) showing Mercury's helmet on an olive branch. It was so called because the helmet seemed to resemble the widely seen ladies' hats of a style referred to as Merry Widow, after the hats worn in Franz Lehar's popular operetta of the day.

Miniature Sheet. See Souvenir Sheet.

Minkus. U.S. and worldwide stamp catalogs of fairly wide usage primarily in the United States. They have been published annually in New York since 1954.

Also see Catalog.

Minor Variety. A stamp with any slight variation from the normal in color, design, or other feature. Some minor varieties are considered significant enough to be accorded separate catalog numbers, but many have differences so slight as to make them merely curiosities, of interest only to specialists in them.

Mint. A stamp in perfect condition exactly as it comes from the post office. Usually the term is applied only to a stamp that is completely untouched—spotless, full original gum, never hinged; otherwise purists prefer the term unused, a more general word describing any stamp that hasn't been postally used. The term commonly appears in abbreviated form, *M* or *m*, often accompanied by *nh*, the abbreviation for never hinged. Often mint stamps are indentified in lists by a star or asterisk, although these symbols simply mean unused, not necessarily mint.

Also see Condition.

Mission Mixture. Unsorted mixed stamps still on paper and sold in bulk, so called because many of them come from missionary societies who accumulate common used stamps in quantity as a means of fund raising.

Also see Bank Mixture; Mixture.

MERRY WIDOW

Mistakes on Stamps. The mistakes considered in this article are limited to those committed by artists or engravers when designing stamps. They do not include errors in printing, which are discussed under other headings (see Error; Invert; Tete-Beche).

Design mistakes have occurred on the stamps of many countries, and are sometimes surprisingly elementary. They are not confined to stamps of the past; seldom does a year go by without one or more new ones being discovered by sharp-eyed collectors among the year's issues. In most cases a mistake is constant through a stamp's entire printing run, or at least through a substantial part of it, and thus doesn't particularly increase the stamp's value. Therefore a fair-sized specialized collection built entirely of mistakes is not impractical for a nominal stamp budget, and such a collection can be of above-average interest as well as being unusual. For clues to finding stamps with mistakes, study the individual notes given in stamp catalogs; and careful study of new issues will now and then turn up a new blunder. But it is important to make certain that what appears to be a design mistake actually is one, for it may not be in every case. In the U.S. Columbian issue of 1893, for instance, a clean-shaven Columbus is shown in sight of land on the one-cent value (230), and a full-bearded Columbus is shown landing the next day on the two-cent value (231), an apparent discrepancy; but the illustrations were from existing paintings, not erroneous creations of the stamps' designers.

Following are examples of design mistakes on stamps. None of them made the affected stamps specially scarce or expensive, except, as noted, the Mauritius misspelling; but even in their correct version the Mauritius stamps are rare. *Argentina, Dominican Republic, Nicaragua.* Argentina erroneously accomplished a paper annexation of the British Falkland Islands and a section of Chile when in 1936 it released a stamp (445) bearing a map of Argentina that showed those areas as belonging to it. Pressure from Britain and Chile brought about a corrected stamp (446) the following year. The error stamp is generally more expensive, but both are common.

Similar map stamps with artist errors in delineating borders have twice caused more serious repercussions; both occurrences were in Central America. In 1900 the Dominican Republic showed on a definitive series (111–119) a map of Hispaniola that seemed to claim certain Haitian territory, and the stamps resulted in border skirmishes between the two countries. And in 1937 a map of Central America on airmail stamps of Nicaragua (C186–C192) showed as Nicaraguan some territory that was in dispute with Honduras; the issue triggered riots by Honduras nationals in Managua, causing some deaths.

Australia. A commemorative issued in 1947 at the one-hundred-fiftieth anniversary of the founding of Newcastle, a city on the Hunter River estuary about one hundred miles north of Sydney, meant to show the estuary's discoverer, Lieutenant John Shortland of the Royal Navy, and is so inscribed. The picture, however, is of the lieutenant's father, Captain John Shortland. The error was never corrected, and the stamp is quite common.

Canada. The illustration on the fifty-cent definitive of 1946 (272) was widely criticized at the time of its issue for careless, and undoubtedly erroneous, depiction of a lumbering operation. The stamp showed a huge tree at the moment it was toppling, while the two loggers who had presumably just cut it were already turned with their backs to it, violating a basic rule of safety and courting a serious or fatal accident. And on the Alexander Graham Bell commemorative of 1947 (274) the portrayed wire-carrying pole that should have been a telephone pole was actually and obviously, so communications people claimed, a telegraph pole. Another illustration error occurred in 1978, when the ice vessel *Chief Justice Robinson* was shown on a fourteen-cent stamp (776) with its flag being windblown in one direction and the smoke from its stack billowing in the opposite direction.

An incorrect accent appeared on the French word *EXPRÈS* on the seventeen-cent airmail special-delivery stamp of 1946 (CE3); instead of the correct grave accent over the second letter *E*, the stamp gave the letter a circumflex accent, forming *EXPRÊS*. Complaints from the French-speaking sector resulted in a corrected version of the stamp appearing a few months later (CE4). Both stamps are fairly common, and are about equal in value.

Another mistake in French happened on the four-stamp 1977 Inuit issue (748–751). The Inuit are Eskimos, and Inuit is an Eskimo word both singular and plural. On all four stamps it appeared in French as Les Inuits with a final *s* incorrectly

115

added, although the English inscription was correct; both English and French are correct on additional Inuit stamps issued in 1978.

East Germany. In 1956 the one-hundredth anniversary of the death of composer Robert Schumann was marked with two stamps (295–296) showing a picture of Schumann and a few lines of his music—only the music was not Schumann's at all, but Franz Schubert's. The faux pas was corrected within a couple of months with two new stamps (303–304) bearing a true Schumann excerpt. There is no significant difference in value between the two issues.

Egypt. The 1874–75 five-para denomination (26 and varieties, including tete-beches) contains the figure 5 upside down in each corner of the stamp. It is believed that this mistake was caused by designer or printer unfamiliarity with arabic numerals, although the figure had appeared correctly on Egyptian stamps as early as the first issues in 1866.

France. In 1937 a stamp commemorating the three-hundredth anniversary of the publication of Rene Descartes's *Discours de la Méthode* incorrectly identified the work as *Discours sur la Méthode* (330). The error was so hotly criticized in France—mislabeling the most celebrated dissertation of the country's most celebrated philosopher—that a corrected stamp (331) was promptly issued. There is little difference in value between the two.

Gambia. Thirteen values of the 1922–27 definitive issue (102–112 and 121–122) bore an illustration of an elephant with impossible hind legs, which were drawn with a joint like a horse's instead of with the trunklike appearance of an elephant's legs. The blunder was particularly noticeable because the elephant is practically a symbol of the country, but it was not corrected until the next definitive series in 1938.

Greece. Sir Edward Codrington, a British commander who assisted the Greek navy at the battle of Navarino in 1827, was honored on a Greek five-drachma stamp (340) at the 1927 centennial of the battle; but the inscription below his picture on the stamp called him Sir Codrington, a nonexistent form of title. The corrected stamp issued in 1928 (341) is several times as expensive as the mistake.

Korea. A long 1951 issue honored with two stamps each the twenty-one countries that were assisting the republic's army in the Korean War. Part of each design was the flag of the honored country. The two stamps for Italy (154–155) erroneously showed the old royal emblem that bore the crown of the House of Savoy, which by that time had long been replaced by a crownless flag. The stamps were reissued with the correct flag in 1952 (154a–155a). None of the four are particularly expensive.

Mauritius. On two of the 1848 two-pence values (4, 6) the denomination appears misspelled as TWO PENOE. Seven cataloged minor varieties of the two numbers carry the mistake, which occurred once on each sheet of twelve stamps. The error is not truly a misspelling, but rather a faulty engraving job that caused the letter *C* to turn into an *O*. The mistakes are in almost every case at least twice as valuable as their correct counterparts, with all of them being rare and some being extremely rare.

Newfoundland. The four-hundredth anniversary of the discovery of Newfoundland was marked in 1897 with a commemorative issue that contains one certain and one probable mistake. The island's discoverer was John Cabot, who is supposedly pictured on the two-cent value (62), but the picture is actually a Holbein portrait of his son Sebastian, also an explorer. A picture of a sailing ship appears on the ten-cent value; it purports to be John Cabot's *Matthew*, but the same picture had been used four years earlier in the U.S. Columbian issue as Columbus's *Santa Maria*, which most experts feel correctly identified it. (A presumably correct picture of the *Matthew* appears on the 1949 Canadian stamp (282) marking the entry of Newfoundland as the tenth province.)

Then in the 1910 issue commemorating the three-hundredth anniversary of colonization, two mistakes appeared on the same six-cent stamp. One was in the picture caption, where Sir Francis Bacon, described in an inscription as a guiding spirit in the colonization scheme, was called Lord Bacon. The other was in the word colonization, which first appeared with the letter Z reversed (92) and later with the letter corrected (92a); the mistake version is generally about double the cost of the corrected version. Sir Francis Bacon remained Lord Bacon on both versions.

Saint Kitts-Nevis. Probably the most persistent of all mistakes on stamps is the anachronism that was pictured on twenty-eight of the first stamps of the British West Indies islands Saint Kitts-Nevis between 1903 and 1929. Then in 1973 the

NEWFOUNDLAND
LORD BACON MISTAKE

same picture was used again, this time on two values (270, 272) of an issue commemorating the seventieth anniversary of the islands' stamps. The unchanging picture showed Christopher Columbus looking for land through a telescope in 1492; but telescopes were not known until early in the seventeenth century.

United States. On the 1940 Pony Express issue (894) one foreleg of the galloping horse was shown bent back at knee and fetlock, a position equine people claimed is never assumed in a gallop. The stamp was widely criticized by horse lovers because of this error.

And when the three-hundred-fiftieth anniversary of the *Mayflower* landing was commemorated on a stamp in 1970 (1420), the British flag pictured flying from the ship's rigging was the modern Union Jack that includes the diagonal red cross of Saint Patrick. But at the time of the Pilgrims this flag was about 180 years off in the future, Saint Patrick's cross not being incorporated into it until 1801, after Ireland became part of the United Kingdom.

Modifications were made in an existing picture for the ten-cent Parcel Post stamp of 1912 (Q6), resulting in a paradoxical illustration. The original picture showed a ship arriving in New York harbor, with Staten Island in the background. For the stamp, Staten Island was replaced with the more interesting background of the New York skyline, which made the ship appear to be leaving the harbor. Then a mail tender was shown meeting the ship—but mail tenders met inbound ships, not outbound ones. Both of these picture changes were needed to create the mistake, which wouldn't have existed if only one of them had been made.

U.S. PARCEL POST MISTAKE

Mixture. A package of unsorted mixed stamps sold in bulk on original paper, and containing many duplicates. Mixtures are inexpensively priced, being made up of accumulations from business organizations, church and mission societies, and similar recipients of large quantities of mail; the accumulations are bought and packaged by stamp wholesalers and dealers for sale to collectors. Since mixtures comprise the commonest stamps, they are mostly used as starter packages by beginners; but they are also of value to specialists studying postmarks or minor varieties in color or design.

Mounting Methods. The earliest method of mounting stamps was simply to stick them directly to the album page. This method was damaging to mint stamps, for it used their original gum; used stamps also suffered, sometimes seriously, depending on what kind of adhesive the collector employed to stick them. The practice persisted well into the twentieth century, although hinges had been introduced many years previously and were used by most serious collectors as early as 1870. Mounts were a much later innovation, having become popular only in fairly recent times.

Hinges. The hinge is the most common means of mounting stamps. It is inexpensive, simple, and practical for all stamps with the one exception that hinging does mar the gum on mint copies and is consequently avoided by most collectors of unused stamps. The biggest improvement in hinges over the years has been peelability, before which hinge remnants had to be soaked off stamps. When opening a new package of hinges marked peelable, however, it is advisable to test them by mounting a stamp overnight and making sure the hinge peels the next day; the fact is that hinges marked peelable are not always actually so.

The mechanics of hinging are too well known to go into here, but a couple of cautions are worth mentioning: First, only minimum moisture should be applied to the hinge, for too much can lessen its peelability and may also cause a permanent pucker on the album page; second, should you make an error in mounting, do not remove the hinge from the stamp or page until it is thoroughly dry, or it will damage the paper fibers instead of coming off clean. (It should also be noted that most experts recommend moistening only the ends of the hinge away from the fold, to allow the stamp to be pulled out a little from the page for examination of the back without bending the perforations. This is advice the average collector can ignore, because it makes the adhering areas too small and the stamp vulnerable to coming off the page at even light handling contact; on the rare occasions when you might have reason to study a stamp's back, it's simple to remove and remount the stamp.)

While the conventional spot for the hinge has always been near the top of the stamp, this position is not always possible with triangular and certain other odd-shaped stamps, and it is not necessarily the best with stamps of exaggerated height. The drawing shows suggested hinge placements for some of these shapes; note that you are looking at the front of the stamps, and at mountings for a right-hand page.

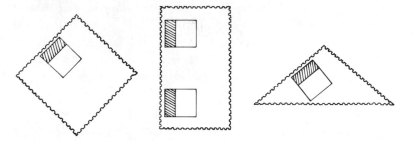

Mounts. Another method of mounting, one that has both advantages and disadvantages, is the use of mounts. Basically a mount comes in the form of a lightweight transparent sleeve that can be opened for inserting the stamp and closes flat to hold the stamp securely; the back is gummed for attachment to the album page. Sleeves are made in various heights to accommodate every size of stamp, and the right height (slightly higher than the stamp) should always be used so the stamp will be held fast but without damage to the perforations; the sleeve is cut to proper width either before or after the stamp is inserted. Most makes also come in individual mounts precut to widths for all stamps, as well as in mounts in sizes large enough for blocks and sometimes covers. Mounts are optionally available with black background, which some collectors prefer for displaying their stamps.

The advantages of mounts include their attractiveness, the protection they give stamps against direct handling, and the fact that they allow unused stamps to be mounted unhinged, a condition that has become something of a fetish among mint collectors. But they add bulk to album pages, they can sometimes be hard to remove, and they're considerably more expensive than hinges, which means they're not usually practical for collections heavy in common stamps. There is also some collector opinion that over a long period mounts can be harmful to stamps, partly because they shut off most air circulation and partly because some kinds of plastic materials used for mounts are felt to cause discoloration or other damaging effects.

120

Other Methods. There are various kinds of albums referred to as hingeless that employ transparent pockets, transparent overlays, or other built-in means of mounting. Such albums are comparatively costly; one typical manufacturer lists his hingeless pages at around three times the price of standard ones. For mint stamps some collectors use stock books as hingeless albums, especially stock books with page-width transparent pockets. For covers a practical and popular mounting method is use of the gummed corners made for mounting photographs in albums.

Also see Stock Book.

Mulreadies. Popular name for the pictorial envelopes (cachets) issued by Great Britain in 1840 in conjunction with the first postage stamp, the Penny Black. They are called after their designer, the British artist William Mulready. They feature a busy drawing of Britannia surrounded by symbolic figures and many kinds of people engaging in various activities, the whole representing the worldwide British Empire. They were printed in black for domestic mail and in blue for overseas mail. Because of the pretentiousness of their design they were widely parodied, and for this reason were withdrawn from circulation after a few months to be replaced by the plain envelopes carrying only an embossed stamp still in use today. Mulreadies have become popular items for collectors of postal stationery, and are now highly sought after.

National Bank Note Company. Printers of the U.S. postage stamps of 1870–71.

Also see Bank Note Issues.

National Parks Issue. U.S. issue of 1934 containing ten varieties from one cent to ten cents (740–749) and depicting various U.S. national parks. The designs were subsequently used again on the special Farley printings and on a few souvenir sheets. The original issue (but not necessarily the subsequent releases) has always been popular with collectors.

Also see Farley Issues; Souvenir Sheet.

Never Hinged. A self-explanatory condition of some unused stamps, widely considered desirable but downgraded by some collectors as an unnecessary fetish. In any case, evidence of hinging—marked or disturbed gum—tends to lower an unused stamp's value. The term commonly appears in its abbreviated form, *NH* or *nh.*

New Carlisle Provisional. The first known stamp of the colony of Canada, a three-penny black issued by the postmaster of New Carlisle, Quebec, in 1851. It is unique and one of Canada's most expensive stamps, although not listed in all catalogs.

Also see Rarities: Canada Postmaster's Provisional.

New-Issue Service. A convenient way for collectors of mint stamps to keep up with new releases as they appear is to subscribe to one of the new-issue services offered by many dealers and government philatelic agencies. Such services automatically send the subscriber new issues according to his standing instructions and within prearranged dollar amounts; often, especially in the case of government agencies, payment is by means of a deduction from an advance deposit account. New-issue services are not approval services, and shipments are generally considered firm sales without return or refund privileges. Governments typically sell their stamps at face value with a handling charge added, while most dealer services sell at a markup over face value. Over two hundred stamp-issuing countries maintain philatelic agencies to serve collectors (or in a few instances, to serve dealers only); addresses for the most popular countries that serve individual collectors are given in section 4, "Philatelic Agencies by Country."

1879 NEWSPAPER ISSUE

Newspaper Stamps. Special stamps issued by many countries for payment of postage, and sometimes tax, on periodicals and other printed matter. Newspaper stamps were used in the United States from 1865 till around 1898, with denominations as high as one hundred dollars (PR1–PR125r); today most values are somewhat scarce, especially in used condition. There have been no newspaper stamps in Canada. A few early Austrian newspaper stamps have become expensive rarities, an unusual status for special-purpose stamps.

Also see Rarities: Austrian Newspaper.

NH, nh. Never hinged (see).

Nonadhesive. A stamp or other postal indicium printed on an envelope, letter sheet, or postcard, as distinguished from a regular gummed stamp. Nonadhesives are usually collected as specialized material, although some printed albums provide spaces for certain of them.

Obsolete. Describes stamps no longer issued but not necessarily invalid for postage. This usually means definitives that have been replaced by a new series, commemoratives that have sold out, types that have been discontinued, or face values no longer serving a postal need. Such stamps remain valid unless they are also demonetized, an action rarely taken except occasionally in a country experiencing a sudden change in government philosophy.

Also see Demonetization.

Off-center. See Centering.

Officials. Stamps issued for official or other government use. They have been used by many countries, sometimes only for short periods of time, and often consist simply of regular stamps overprinted for the purpose. Official stamps are not used as widely as they once were, partly because of franking, which dispenses with stamps entirely. They are obsolete in both the United States and Canada.

United States. Official stamps were introduced in 1873, with individual types for nine government departments: agriculture, executive, interior, justice, navy, post office, state, treasury, war. In 1879 they were replaced by existing official envelopes, which themselves were replaced by franked envelopes in 1884, at which time the official stamps and envelopes were both declared obsolete. Most of the stamps (O1–O120) are fairly common used or unused, but a few are scarce or comparatively rare.

Canada. The first official stamps were regular stamps with perforated initials; in this form they are not listed by all catalogs. In 1949 they were superseded by regular stamps overprinted first with O.H.M.S. (On His Majesty's Service) and later with G (Government). There were also two each of airmail and special-delivery officials. Official stamps were discontinued entirely in 1963 in favor of printed indicia to free government departments from carrying stamps in stock. With a few exceptions the officials are common both unused and used.

Also see Franking; Indicia; Overprint; Perfins.

Off Paper. Describes used stamps that have been soaked and removed from the envelope or other cover to which they had been gummed.

Offset Lithography. See Printing Methods and How to Distinguish Them.

OG, og. Original gum (see Gum).

O.H.M.S. Abbreviation for On His (or Her) Majesty's Service, an overprint or perforated initials used on certain Canadian official stamps, as well as on official stamps of Great Britain and other British Commonwealth countries.

Also see Officials.

Omahas. Popular name for the 1898 Trans-Mississippi Exposition issue of the U.S. (285–293), so called because the site of the exposition was Omaha, Nebraska. The set is a handsome one with its typical scenes of western emigration, the one-dollar black showing cattle in a storm (292) often being called the most beautiful of all U.S. stamps.

Omnibus Issue. A group of stamps issued by different countries but marking the same event or theme. The stamps often carry a similar or even identical design. Examples of omnibus issues include the Europa series produced by various cooperating European countries, which have appeared annually since 1956 and each year feature a common theme, and such British Commonwealth series as the Silver Jubilee issues of Elizabeth II in 1977. Sometimes a worldwide occasion—the International Cooperation Year in 1965 is an example—prompts stamp issues from several countries; these emissions are occasionally referred to as omnibus issues, but actually they are not if produced independently of each other without interrelating effort among the countries.

Also see Europa; Jubilee.

On Cover, On Paper. Describes a used stamp still gummed to its envelope (cover) or just a piece of it (paper); most stamps in bulk mixtures are on paper.

Original Gum. See Gum.

Overprint. Any printed matter added to a stamp on top of its original design. Overprints are frequently used and can serve any of several purposes including commemorative, as on the U.S. Discovery of Hawaii issue of 1928 (647–648); change of a stamp's function (most of Canada's official stamps are regular issues overprinted O.H.M.S. or G); or special needs, as on the U.S. Kansas and Nebraska issues of 1929. An overprint is also often used to change a stamp's face value, in which case it is more correctly described as a surcharge.

Also see Kansas and Nebraska Issues; Surcharge.

Oxidization. See Renovating Soiled or Damaged Stamps.

Pacific Steam Navigation Company. The first stamps of Peru (1–2), issued in 1857, were actually stamps that had been prepared ten years earlier by the Pacific Steam Navigation Company and bore only the company's identification without the country name; they were the only private stamps ever to become a nation's official postal issue. The company's intention had been for the stamps to pay postage on mail carried on its vessels, but it operated in Peru's offshore waters and the Peruvian government objected; consequently the stamps were never put to their intended use and instead were eventually turned over to Peru for its own introduction of postal service. They were superseded within about three months with regular government emissions and thus are scarce, especially in used condition.

Packets and How They Are Priced. Stamp packets consist of stamps all different and removed from paper ready for album mounting, as opposed to mixtures, which are heavy in duplication and usually with the stamps still on paper. The stamps in a packet can be worldwide or representative of a single country, group of countries, or topical theme; they can be in either unused or used condition, but if unused they are more likely to have been produced for collectors than for postal needs. All dealers sell packets, and the catalogs of mail-order dealers who specialize in them (you can find them through their ads in the stamp periodicals) often list thousands of different ones containing small to large quantities. Packets seldom contain anything but common stamps, but they are the best source for starting any worldwide, country, or topical collection.

Pricing. A typical dealer price list might show U.S. used stamps roughly as follows: 300 for $2, 500 for $7, 700 for $12, 1,000 for $30. Note how the stamps cost proportionately more as the packets get bigger. The reason is that there are only so many of the cheaper stamps, and as additional varieties are added they must necessarily include more and more increasingly expensive numbers. For the same reason two packets of 500, even from different dealers, will mostly duplicate each other—they won't approximate a single

125

packet of 1,000. Thus in buying a packet you should always get as big a one as you can, after which there is little point in buying further packets of the same country.

Pair. Two stamps unseparated from each other. Although they may be joined together either horizontally or vertically, the term is usually taken to mean the horizontal form.

Pane. Strictly, the sheet of stamps sold at the post office is not a sheet at all, but a pane; a sheet is the form in which stamps come off the printing press, and it typically contains four panes separated by gutters. The sheet is cut to make the panes, the form in which the stamps are sold. This distinction in meaning, however, is not invariably observed, nor is there any real reason to observe it; what is strictly a pane will probably always be popularly called a sheet. A pane is also a complete page from a stamp booklet, and very often this is what is meant when the term is used.

Also see Booklet.

Paper Types and How to Distinguish Them. Special types of paper are not as widely used today for printing stamps as they were in the past. In earlier stamp-issuing days there was considerable experimenting to find the best paper for gum compatibility, perforated strength, resistance to fraudulent reuse, and other desirable characteristics. Sometimes identical stamps were printed on differing types of paper and have been given separate catalog listings, often with significant price variances. In such instances the ability to identify paper types is important, even though in most cases the average collector has little need to do so. Descriptions of the most frequently used papers follow.

Batonné. A lightweight paper, wove or laid, used mostly for international postal stationery but also appearing occasionally as stamp stock. Crisp, thin, with parallel watermarked lines a quarter-inch or so apart.

Bond. A strong mediumweight paper, usually wove, appearing in various forms and designed to resist ink penetration. It was used for many early stamps of the United States. Hard textureless surface.

Chalky. A somewhat glossy paper employed to discourage fraudulent reuse of stamps. Because it has a chalky surface with little integrity, any attempt to remove the postmark will also dislodge the surface and thus remove stamp design. It can be readily identified by lightly scratching it with a coin, which will leave a dark mark. Caution: Stamps on chalky paper should not be soaked; paper remnants should be carefully floated off or sweated off (see Removing Paper from Stamps).

Granite. A wove paper containing haphazard tiny threads of various colors, giving a look similar to the random pattern of granite. Granite paper was mainly used as a deterrent to forgery, and is readily identifiable by its appearance.

Laid. One of the two major classifications of paper, the other being wove; all paper types are either one or the other, and some are made in both forms. In the manufacture of laid paper, close parallel lines are impressed in the pulp with wire cloth. These lines give the translucent effect of a watermark (which actually they are) and are easily seen when the paper is held to the light.

Pelure. A crisp, lightweight, translucent paper, either wove or laid. A printed design on pelure shows through to the back of the paper.

Rep, Repp, Ribbed. A paper with close parallel ridges on one or both sides. The ridges, or ribs, are extremely fine but can often be sensed or felt by lightly sliding a fingernail over the surface.

Silk. A wove paper containing imbedded silk threads, either random short ones similar to granite paper or long ones extending across the paper but not necessarily parallel or even in a straight line. Like granite, silk paper was used for security purposes, and it is also visually identifiable by its described appearance.

Wove. The second major classification of paper, and overall more generally used than laid. Fine wire gauze is used in the manufacture of wove paper, giving it a closely textured body with no visible built-in pattern like the parallel lines of laid. Most of today's stamps are printed on wove paper of one kind or another.

Par Avion. (French) by plane. This phrase is an accepted international standard on air labels to instruct forwarding by airmail.

Also see Air Label.

Parcel Post Stamps. Several countries have issued stamps for parcel post, the 1913 U.S. series of twelve values (Q1–Q12) being the best known. These stamps remain the only parcel-post stamps ever issued by the United States (none have been issued by Canada). They were to be used on all parcel post in an effort to keep track of receipts for this service for

PARCEL POST

127

balancing against the cost of rendering it, but for real or imagined reasons their acceptance was resisted by postal employees. A few months after their introduction their use on regular mail was authorized until stocks were exhausted, and no further printings were made. A set of five parcel-post-due stamps issued concurrently (JQ1–JQ5) were also soon discontinued. The issues are popular with collectors, however, and contain no scarcities, all but a few values being quite common.

The twelve parcel-post stamps were printed in carmine rose and carried identical designs except for the pictures, eight of which showed postal operations and modes of forwarding, the other four showing urban or rural industry. The twenty-cent value (Q8) picturing an aeroplane carrying mail has the distinction of being the first stamp ever to have a plane in its design, while the ten-cent value (Q6) has the negative distinction of an error in its illustration of a ship in New York harbor (see Mistakes on Stamps: U.S.A.).

Peace Bridge. This international span crossing the Niagara River between Buffalo, New York, and Fort Erie, Ontario, is of note philatelically for having been the subject, on its fiftieth anniversary in 1977, of simultaneously issued but non-identical commemorative stamps by both the United States (1721) and Canada (737).

Also see Saint Lawrence Seaway.

Pelure Paper. See Paper Types and How to Distinguish Them.

Pen Cancel. In many countries postage stamps have served also as revenue stamps, in which case they have been canceled with means other than postmarks, often simply by hand with a pen; but in early stamp-issuing days a few countries also canceled postage stamps by pen until their postmarks were developed. For these reasons pen-canceled stamps may or may not have been used postally; the only way to prove postal use of a stamp that could also have served for revenue is to leave it on its cover.

PENCE ISSUE

Pence Issues. The term refers to Canada's first stamps (1–13) issued in sterling denominations between 1851 and 1859 before the country adopted the dollar as standard. All of the pence issues are scarce, a few are rare, and one, the twelve-pence Chalon of 1851 (3), is Canada's second most expensive stamp.

Also see Rarities: Canada Twelve-Pence Chalon.

Penny Black. Popular name for the world's first postage stamp, the black one-penny value (1) issued by Great Britain in May 1840 under the authorization of Sir Rowland Hill (see Hill, Sir Rowland), a Treasury official. A two-penny blue stamp (2) was issued one day later, so there were actually two world's firsts, but the honor has traditionally been accorded just to the Penny Black. The stamps were identical in design and bore a cameo-style profile of the young Queen Victoria, who had acceded to the throne only three years earlier; the portrait was such a favorite of the queen that it remained on British stamps throughout her long reign ending in 1901, although several British Commonwealth countries including Canada used more contemporary likenesses as she aged. The stamps didn't show the country name, which was considered unnecessary since in 1840 there were no other countries with postage stamps; that established a precedent that still exists—Great Britain is the only country whose name doesn't appear on its stamps.

In 1841, the year after its appearance, the Penny Black was replaced by a reddish version (3) which became known as the Penny Red and was in use until 1880, issued in shades of red and red-brown in several cataloged varieties and minor varieties. The reason for the change was that the Penny Black had to be canceled with a colored postmark, which was washable and opened the door to fraudulent reuse, while indelible black ink could be used for the red stamp's cancellation. Despite its relatively short issue life the Penny Black is fairly common in used condition even today. With these two one-penny issues, and in 1841 a second version (4) of the two-penny blue as well, Great Britain actually issued the world's first four stamps before Brazil in 1843 became the second stamp-issuing country.

In Britain in 1839, while postage still had to be paid in person by sender or addressee, around 75 million pieces of mail were processed; in 1840, with the Penny Black in use for only about eight months, this figure more than doubled, and by 1845 it had quadrupled to over 300 million. By 1850, moreover, around twenty countries including the United States had commenced issuing postage stamps, and by 1860 the number was nearing one hundred. Most of the credit for this spectacular increase in postal communications must go to the convenience and simplicity of the postage stamp as exemplified in the Penny Black.

Penny Red. See Penny Black.

Perf. Perforated (see Perforation).

Perfins. Perforated initials in stamps, the letters usually representing a business organization, an institution or society, or any other large user of postage. The first perfins were authorized in Great Britain in 1868 for antitheft purposes. The large quantities of stamps needed on hand by business firms were a target for pilferage, since the stamps could be sold back to the post office by anyone at a small discount; but the perforated initials established corporate ownership and rendered the stamps not further salable—and hence not redeemable—by the post office. Perfins were soon in use throughout much of Europe, first appeared in Canada in 1889, and were authorized in the United States in 1908. They have also been used by government departments as a means of making official stamps from regular ones. They appear less frequently today than formerly, since antitheft security is served more efficiently by the stamp collector's bugbear, the postage meter, and government purposes are more easily met by printed envelope indicia. Perfins generally lower a stamp's price, which is considered one of their attractions by the many collectors who specialized in them.

Perforation. The first perforated stamps appeared in Great Britain in 1853, and next in Sweden in 1855. Perforating was adopted by the United States in 1857 and by Canada in 1858, with other countries gradually following throughout the 1860s. Most modern stamps are perforated by one of three methods: line, comb, or harrow. Line (also called guillotine) perforating punches straight lines in one direction on the sheet, and then in the other direction. Comb perforating punches three sides of all the stamps in a row with one stroke; it takes its name from the punch's resemblance to a comb, with one straight line across the row and teeth at right angles spaced the width of a stamp apart and projecting the height of a stamp. Harrow perforating punches the entire pattern in one operation; it is used largely for souvenir sheets and other small panes.

During most of the nineteenth century there was considerable experimenting with perforation sizes—that is, the number of perforation holes within a given length—to provide the easiest separation without unduly weakening the paper structure; and with paper types themselves also being tested, this often meant changing the perforation size, frequently on the same stamp design. Hence it soon became necessary to establish a measurement criterion, and in 1866 Dr. J. A. LeGrand, a French physician and philatelist, proposed that size be stated as the number of perforation holes in the length of two centimeters, which has been the standard ever since. Thus perf.12 in a stamp's description means twelve holes in two centimeters, not twelve holes along the stamp's edge. Compound perforations—two different ones on the same stamp—are common; they are shown, for instance, as perf.11x12, in which example the perforation is eleven top and bottom and twelve on the sides, the horizontal figure always being given first. Perforation size can easily be measured with a perforation gauge (see), although it is not really of significance except for identifying stamps issued in more than one size. Such stamps are not limited to early ones, for perforation differences can occur on otherwise identical stamps even today; for example, six of the higher values on the Canadian definitive series introduced in 1973 (586–601) were issued with two different perforation sizes in addition to other minor dissimilarities.

Perforation Gauge. A device for measuring perforations on a stamp. It is simply a scale made of light metal or cardboard, with perforation patterns printed on it to exact size for the stamp edge to be laid over and matched against. In buying this inexpensive accessory choose one that has the scales printed at its edges as well as down the center; center scales are easiest for measuring unmounted stamps, and edge scales easiest for mounted stamps, as they can be slipped under the stamps without removing the stamps from the page. There are also gauges made of transparent plastic, to be laid over the stamp; these should have the printing on their underside so the scale will be directly on the stamp to prevent a parallax effect through the thickness of the plastic.

Personal Delivery Stamps. Stamps issued by Czechoslovakia between 1937 and 1946 (EX1–EX3) and the Czech provinces of Bohemia and Moravia in 1939 (EX1–EX2), their purpose being to guarantee delivery only to the actual addressee of a letter or other mailed matter.

Philately. The broad term used to describe all aspects of the collecting and study of postage stamps and other postal material, and also the study of postal history. The word was coined by Georges Herpin, a French collector, in the nineteenth century, and derives from the Greek *philos* (love) and *ateleia* (exemption from tax), the latter referring to prepayment by stamp. It is pronounced phi-lat'-e-ly with a short *a*, and a collector is a phi-lat'-e-list; but note that philatelic is pronounced phil-a-tel'-ic.

Phosphorescence. See Luminescence.

Photoengraving. See Printing Methods and How to Distinguish Them.

Photogravure. See Printing Methods and How to Distinguish Them.

Photolithography. See Printing Methods and How to Distinguish Them.

Pictorials. Stamps whose design is an illustration other than a portrait of an individual. Although today's stamps are mostly pictorials or portraits, plain typeset designs and coats of arms were common on earlier issues.

Pigeon Post. There have been one or two documented but minor instances of pigeons being used to transport messages for private postal services issuing their own stamps. But the best-known example of pigeon post took place in 1870 during the siege of Paris in the Franco-Prussian War. Pigeons were sporadically carried out of Paris to Tours by manned balloons, which also carried mail out. In Tours the pigeons were released to fly home, bearing messages. There were no postage stamps involved in the operation, but a few of the messages still exist and are extremely valuable although without philatelic recognition.

Also see Balloon Mail.

Pilgrim Tercentenary Issue. A three-stamp set of the United States (548–550) issued in 1920 to mark the three hundredth anniversary of the pilgrims' landing at Plymouth, and of note because the stamps were the first U.S. emissions that showed neither country name nor initials.

Plate Block. A block of four or more stamps unseparated from the part of the sheet margin that shows the number of the plate used in the printing. On U.S. multicolor stamps several plate numbers appear on the margin, usually placed far enough apart that several stamps are required in one direction to include them all. Plate blocks are popular with many collectors, and because there are fewer of them than of ordinary blocks, they are priced at a premium. Generally they are collected unused.

Also see Block.

Plating. The reconstructing of an entire sheet of stamps with each stamp in the position it occupied on the unseparated sheet, a specialized branch of philately. Reconstruction is relatively easy with the pre-1887 stamps of Great Britain, since they bear corner letters identifying their horizontal row and position across in the row. It becomes a challenge, however, with other stamps, where no such identification appears. But plating experts, by means of deduction and infinitesimal differences from stamp to stamp, are often able to complete sheets, particularly those of older issues when during the engraving and printing processes flaws often appeared or retouching was done on individual stamps or parts of plates.

Also see Corner Letters.

Pony Express Stamps. Private stamps issued in 1861 by Wells, Fargo & Co. for payment of mail forwarded by the famous Pony Express, for which the stagecoach company was an agent. The Pony Express was a privately owned enterprise, not a government service, that for five dollars per half ounce (later reduced to a dollar) carried mail between Saint Joseph, Missouri, and Sacramento, California, with 190 way stations for changing horses and riders. It started in April 1860 and ran until October 1861, when completion of the first transcontinental telegraph line ended its usefulness. The Pony Express stamps, which are rare and much sought after by students of postal history, have been extensively forged; at least one value—a three dollar stamp existing in several different colors—is completely bogus.

Pony Express riders have been the subjects of four U.S. stamps: the two-cent value of the definitive issues of 1869 and 1875 (113, 124), the 1940 Pony Express Eightieth Anniversary commemorative (894), and the 1960 Pony Express Centennial commemorative (1154).

Also see Wells, Fargo & Co.

Poor. A grade of stamp condition. For definitions of recognized grades, see Condition.

Port Hood Provisionals. Cut portions of the three-cent value of the Canada 1898 definitive issue (78) surcharged to either one cent (88B) or two cents (88C), the former being on a vertical third of the cut stamp, the latter on a vertical two-thirds. They were used briefly in 1899 at Port Hood, Nova Scotia, because of a local shortage of the regular one-cent and two-cent values, but are not recognized by all catalogs because they were not officially authorized. They are scarce both unused and used.

Also see Bisect.

Postage-Due Stamps. These special stamps are used by most countries for collecting from the addressee any shortage in the amount of postage paid by the sender's stamps, the postage-dues being affixed to the cover by the post office and the indicated amount being collected by the delivering letter carrier. In the United States, postage meters have supplanted the stamps in many post offices, causing a decrease in the supply of used copies; to counteract this, current postage dues are often canceled to order for the philatelic trade.

Also see Canceled to Order.

U.S. POSTAGE DUE

Postage Meter. This mail-franking device, which was introduced in the United States and first authorized for use in 1920, has now almost entirely replaced stamps among business firms. At the user's need meters are set and sealed by the post office to dispense a total prepaid amount of postage. They can be keyed by the user to print any amount at a time, the amount being printed along with place and date on the envelope as it is fed through the meter. A slogan or other promotional phrase can be added to the imprint if desired. The machine also prints and dispenses postage tapes for affixing to parcels and other bulky pieces. Although most collectors deplore the universal use of meters—especially by U.S. post offices, where they have widely replaced postage-due and other special-purpose stamps as well as the high values used on parcel post—there are others who collect meter imprints and tapes as a specialized branch of philately.

Postal Card. Strictly, a postal card is a government-issue message card with printed stamp, as distinguished from a commercial picture post card.

Postal History. A branch of philately embracing everything relative to the origins and development of postal operations from ancient times to the present. Stamps, covers, and postal documents and stationery are the main components of postal-history collections. Supporting studies include routings, postmarks, and special services.

Postal Stationery. Items of stationery sold in post offices and bearing an imprinted postage stamp. Such items include envelopes, postal cards, self-mailable letter sheets, and wrappers. Postal stationery is collected either as part of a general collection or as its own specialty.

Postmark. Broadly, any postally significant marking on a stamp or cover, but the term is most often limited in meaning to the cancellation, specifically the portion of the cancellation bearing the name of the originating post office and the date; the marks of destination office and in-transit forwarding offices also sometimes appear, particularly on early covers. On many covers the postmark is a more important determinant of value than the stamp; this is especially true in the case of early first day covers and those bearing a relationship to an important event.

Also see Cancellation; First Day Cover.

Postmasters' Provisionals. Stamps issued by local postmasters, usually for limited periods of time and valid only on mail posted within the postmaster's jurisdiction. The term is generally taken to mean the postmasters' provisionals of the United States (1X1–11X8), which were in use from 1845 until 1847 when the first government stamps appeared; although they could be used only in the place of issue they were valid for prepayment of postage anywhere in the country, as opposed to locals, which paid only for local delivery. Almost all of the U.S. postmasters' provisionals are rare, a few of them being extremely so.

The provisionals were issued in the following cities and towns: Alexandria, Virginia; Annapolis and Baltimore, Maryland; Boscawen, New Hampshire; Brattleboro, Vermont; Lockport and New York, New York; Millbury, Massachusetts; New Haven, Connecticut; Providence, Rhode Island; St. Louis, Missouri. A postmaster's envelope was issued in Tuscumbia, Alabama (12XU1).

Two provisional issues have appeared in Canada, one at New Carlisle, Quebec, in 1851, and a set of two stamps at Port Hood, Nova Scotia, in 1899. Neither issue has attained universal catalog recognition, although the New Carlisle stamp, which is unique, is one of Canada's highest-priced rarities.

Also see Confederate States Provisionals; Locals; Rarities; U.S. Postmasters' Provisionals, Canada Postmaster's Provisional.

Post Office Mauritius. Popular name for the extremely rare first two stamps of Mauritius (1–2) issued in 1847, so called because the words POST OFFICE appeared on them in apparent error; subsequent issues carried the words POST PAID.

Also see Rarities: Post Office Mauritius.

U.S. PRECANCEL

Precancel. A stamp with printed cancellation applied by the post office before its sale. Precancels are used in mass mailings by business firms and other organizations, such mailings being delivered in bulk to the post office, where they bypass further cancellation and thus save processing time. They originated around the time of World War I and are common in many countries. In the United States a precancellation consists of the name of the city and state prominently overprinted on the stamp with a black horizontal line above and below it; it can be applied in the city of origin, in which case it is called a local precancel, or by the Bureau of Printing and Engraving, when it is called a bureau precancel. Canada at first used a similar type of overprint, but in 1931 changed to an identifying number for the city of origin, and later to horizontal lines only. Precancel collecting is an organized branch of philately in which the stamps themselves, being mostly low-denomination definitives, are of less importance than the imprint of the issuing city; instead of stamp varieties, which are limited, the collector seeks city imprints.

PRESIDENTIALS DESIGN

Presidentials. Popular name for the U.S. definitive issue of 1938 (803–834) consisting of thirty-two denominations from half-cent to five dollars. The series showed in chronological order all the presidents of the United States through Calvin Coolidge along with their dates of office, as well as Benjamin Franklin, Martha Washington, and the White House. The Presidentials are of simple, pleasing, and uniformly organized design, the portraits being in the form of classic busts. They have always enjoyed wide collector popularity.

Prestamp Covers. Envelopes and other postal stationery used before adhesive postage stamps were introduced. To be of philatelic value they must bear evidence of actual postal use.

Primes. Popular name for a recurrent Canadian series commemorating past prime ministers as follows: 1951 issue, Borden and King (303–304); 1952, Abbott and Mackenzie (318–319); 1954, Thompson and Bowell (349–350); 1955, Bennett and Tupper (357–358); 1961, Meighen (393). The term does not include the 1927 issues on which Sir John A. Macdonald and Sir Wilfred Laurier appeared singly (142, 144) and together (147), or the 1973 definitive issue showing prime ministers on seven low values (586–592).

Printing Methods and How to Distinguish Them. Correct identification of a stamp sometimes depends on being able to recognize the method by which it was printed. Occasionally in earlier days stamps otherwise identical were printed by more than one method, giving them separate catalog listings often with significant price variances. While generally speaking the average collector seldom needs to identify printing methods, in those instances the ability to do so is important. It is also helpful to recognize processes that leave a vulnerability; for example, water or watermark-detecting liquid may possibly damage photogravure printing. Following are various methods used in printing stamps; the suggested ways to recognize them are effective in most cases, but sometimes because of obscure differences positive identification requires expert opinion.

Engraving. In this process the design is cut into a steel block by the engraver and reproduced in multiples onto a printing plate by means of a process named for Jacob Perkins, an American-turned-Briton, who invented it in the early nineteenth century (for an outline of the process, see Engraving under E). The printing plate is in incised (intaglio) form like the original engraving, and the ink is held in the depressed engraved lines and deposited on the paper in minutely raised relief. Engraving lines are clean and sharp. Sometimes their raised effect can be seen under a powerful magnifier or felt by running a fingernail lightly over the design. The easiest way to identify an engraved stamp, however, is to rub an ordinary piece of foil wrap over it; this should bring out the entire raised design, usually recognizable even if faint.

Flat Plate. Describes a type of printing press, not a printing method. Flat plate refers to a flatbed press, as opposed to a rotary press.

Heliogravure. A type of photogravure, little used in printing or stamp production today.

Intaglio. Any printing process (engraving, for instance) where the image to be inked and printed is recessed into the plate, the design thereby appearing on the paper in relief. Formerly also called copperplate. Pronounced in-tal'-yo.

Letterpress. In philately, synonymous with typography (see).

Line Engraving. Another name for engraving.

Lithography. Originally, printing from a stone plate on which only the design accepts the ink, which is of an oily base; the clear areas within and around the design reject the ink by being kept moist with water. The design is transferred from the plate to paper by contact pressure. See Offset Lithography.

Offset Lithography. This is the modern and universally used method of lithographing, based on the principle that oil and water do not mix (see Lithography). A plate usually of metal and thin enough to curve around a drum carries the image, which is transferred by revolving contact pressure to a rubber blanket also on a drum, and then from the drum to the paper. Because of the intermediate (blanket) impression, the plate carries the image exactly as it will appear printed, not mirror backwards as in direct plate-to-paper methods. Lithographing leaves no raised or embossed effect, and is most easily distinguished by examination under a magnifying glass; illustrations have a pattern of fine dots or drawn lines, or both, which when magnified reveal varying degrees of precision and symmetry, often with small blank areas where dots appear to be missing or lines do not quite meet. Smooth paper is characteristically used for lithography.

Photoengraving. A method of producing illustration plates for use in letterpress or typographic printing in which the design appears in relief on the plate. It is a production step, not a printing process. The term is often misleading because the incised areas on the plate are the nonprint areas, not the ink-carrying design areas as in regular engraving.

Photogravure. In photogravure the design is photographed through an extremely fine screen to form a dotted image which is transferred to a metal printing plate in intaglio form. Thus photogravure, like engraving, produces a printed design in relief; but the relief effect is not defined enough to be felt or leave an impression on a foil rubbing. Like lithography, photogravure is most easily identified by studying its dot structure under a magnifying glass. The dots are evenly sized and spaced, and fine to the point of sometimes being almost invisible; these characteristics are what mainly distinguish photogravure from lithography. Care should be taken in removing paper from photogravure stamps, as soaking the stamps in water can cause their ink to run.

Photolithography. Offset lithography in which the printing plates are made photographically (which practically speaking means virtually all offset lithography).

Rotary Press. Like flat plate, describes a type of printing press, not a printing method. In a rotary press the printing plate is curved around a drum, which stretches the plate images very slightly in the direction of the curve. Stamps printed by the rotary method are about a millimeter larger in one dimension than they would be if printed by a flatbed press. The size difference is demonstrated in the U.S. definitive series of 1922 and its various additional issues, in which certain identical stamps were printed by both methods and carry different catalog numbers; they are easily told apart by size.

Rotogravure. Another name for photogravure, referring specifically to photogravure printed on a rotary press.

Typography. Printing from a raised design, the opposite of intaglio. The ink is applied to the surface of the design and transferred by contact to the paper in much the same way as a rubber stamp works. Typography sometimes leaves a depression in the paper, especially where lettering appears, that can show up on a foil rubbing of the stamp's back; but this condition is not unfailing and cannot always be counted on as a means of identification. Under a magnifier typography seldom shows the minute imperfections common in lithography; and a typographed stamp can be on rough paper, while lithography is almost invariably on smooth paper. Because of the scarcity and fallibility of guidelines, typography is the most difficult printing method for the average collector to identify with certainty.

Private Treaty. A negotiated agreement commonly used as a means of privately selling stamp collections or individual stamps of value, as distinguished from public selling at auction or through a mail-sale catalog. A private-treaty sale is usually arranged by a dealer acting as a commission broker between seller and buyer, who may never meet.

Also see Selling a Stamp Collection.

Pro Juventute. (Latin) for youth. The phrase appears on the semipostal stamps of Switzerland that except for 1914 have been issued annually since 1913 to provide funds for services for the country's children and young people.

Prominent Americans Issue. U.S. definitive series beginning in 1965 and containing values from one cent to five dollars picturing six presidents and thirteen other variously distinguished Americans (1278–1295). The issue is not widely popular, for two main reasons: Several of its subjects, while they may merit a commemorative stamp, hardly seem to belong on a long-lived definitive issue; and the stamps themselves are mostly unattractive, and are unrelated in design.

Proofs. Prints of stamps made for checking purposes during the production process. They include engraver's proofs, for checking the engraving; die proofs, for checking the master die made from the engraving; plate proofs, for checking the completed plate made from the die in multiples; and various other proofs for checking color integrity, registration accuracy, and similar everyday printing matters. Proofs often find their way onto the philatelic market and are sought by some collectors as specialties.

Protecting Stamp Collections from Theft. Stamp collections have a special vulnerability to theft for the simple reason that stamps are almost as good as cash to a thief. Since most dealers are as interested in buying as in selling, there is a ready market for any stamp of value except the well-known pedigreed rarities. The risk of theft has become significant enough that many members of philatelic clubs and organizations do not allow their address to be shown in published membership rosters, and many collectors who formerly exhibited regularly at shows have discontinued the practice because they don't want the attendant publicity for their collections.

In protecting against theft, the ordinary precautions like adequate home security at all times should of course be observed, as should care when transporting stamps by private car or public carrier. And there are specific other precautions a collector should take:

1. Do not tell strangers you are a collector, or discuss philately or stamp organizations with someone you don't know; professional thieves know what's readily exchangeable for cash, they burglarize with advance knowledge of what they'll find, and they work at getting advance knowledge from prospective victims, who usually give it unwittingly. One of the ways they get information is by posing as researchers; always use caution in giving personal and hobby information to a researcher unless you are certain of his—or her—credentials.

2. Do not consign philatelic publications to the trash without removing your address label from the cover; in fact it's best to find some other way of disposal than putting them out for anyone to find, a precaution that also goes for most other types of hobby publications.

3. Do not seek publicity about your philatelic achievements—another precaution that also goes for other hobbies. Your picture in the paper today could mean a thief in your home tomorrow.

4. Do not leave philatelic materials in the house when you're away on vacation, any more than you'd leave cash or securities. The safest place for a valuable collection is in a bank safety deposit box. Some banks have box sizes large enough to hold albums, although the boxes usually rented by individuals will accommodate only unmounted stamps. Check also your bank's safekeeping plan, including its liability policy; you may be able to leave a sealed package of albums in its custody. A home safe is almost useless, for if a burglar can't force it open right on the premises he'll simply cart it off with him; even if it's built in it's not likely to be impregnable against forceful removal. (Actually the security of a bank is desirable at all times for almost any collection of consequence, but since stamps have to be where they can be worked with and viewed if they're to be truly enjoyed, such security is usually—and understandably—shunned by the average collector.)

5. Do not leave philatelic materials in an unattended automobile including the locked trunk. Not only are cars easy break-ins for professionals, but stamp insurance doesn't cover theft from an unattended automobile.

6. Finally, identify your collection thoroughly, a procedure that may act as some deterrent to a thief but is recommended mostly as an important aid to recovery if the collection is ever stolen. Its deterrent value lies in the fact that a thief unversed in stamp collecting is often apparently hesitant to remove mounted stamps from their pages, for many collections that have been stolen are offered for sale intact. Your name and address should appear in indelible ink on every album page, stock-book page, and stamp or cover container. Such identification needn't be unattractive, especially if applied with a small neat rubber stamp or by the use of mail name-and-address labels sealed on with transparent tape.

Another means of identification is microfilm, a single small roll of which is able to carry hundreds of album-page photographs that can be seen blown up through a microfilm viewer. Microfilming is a service commercially available in cities and most large towns at a cost generally reasonable at least for collections containing more than just the commonest varieties. In selecting a firm to film your pages, avoid one that uses rotary equipment and be sure proper lighting is available to capture all aspects of each stamp—white perforations against a white album page, for example. To save time, and hence cost, remove in advance any blank or interleaving sheets from the album; and place a small card on each page showing your name, the date of filming, and any other pertinent data. The finished film roll, which also serves as an inventory record, should like any other inventory be kept in a safe place somewhere apart from the collection.

Rarities. Of the many rare stamps of the world, a few have achieved some degree of fame among collectors often because of something unusual about their history (how they came about, where they were used, how they were discovered), but often, too, for no apparent distinction apart from their rarity. A stamp can also gain status because of its owners; a few of the noted collectors of the past whose association with a stamp helped establish its reputation include Maurice Burrus, Alfred H. Caspary, Theodore Champion, Count Phillippe Ferrari, Colonel Edward H. R. Green, Arthur Hind, and Alfred F. Lichtenstein.

Today it is becoming more and more common for the owner of a valuable stamp to remain anonymous. A principal

142

reason for this is security; a well-known stamp is almost its own insurance against being salable by anyone except the legitimate owner, but that doesn't rule out stealing it and holding it for ransom. Besides, a thief recognizes that wherever there is such a stamp there are also many other valuable ones.

Rarity alone does not cause a stamp to soar in price. To push it into five or six figures, there must be competition to own it. That is why a rare stamp can stay at a comparatively modest price forever, and often does if it's from a country that generates little interest among collectors. It is also why classic U.S. and Canadian stamps are likely to realize more at auction in their home countries where interest in them is high than they would, say, at a European sale.

The following list is representative, not definitive, of philately's best-known rarities. After leading off with the world's most expensive stamp it is in rough order of descending value—rough, because for stamps that seldom change hands value can only be estimated, and a dollar figure is given only in a few cases where it is verifiable. To show broad relative values, asterisks are added to the stamp's catalog number as follows: **** for above $50,000; *** for $25,000–$50,000; ** for $10,000–$25,000; * for below $10,000 (but never much below). If a stamp is rare both used and unused, the asterisks reflect the higher value of the two.

British Guiana Magenta. This is the most valuable stamp in the world. It is the British Guiana one-cent denomination of 1856 (13****), actually a local provisional issued to meet a temporary shortage, and only one copy of it is known. It was printed in black, but gets its name from its magenta paper. It is used, worn, and of unprepossessing design partly obscured by heavy validating initials, but it boasts philatelically famous past owners including Count Ferrari and Arthur Hind, the latter obtaining it by outbidding Britain's King George V at auction. In 1970 it was sold to a syndicate for $280,000, and by the late 1970s the asking price was believed to be in the neighborhood of $1 million. The British Guiana four-cent blue (16**) from the same provisional issue is also comparatively rare but ranks nowhere near the Magenta in value.

Sweden Orange. Only one copy is known of the Sweden Orange, which has been considered Europe's most valuable stamp and was sold in 1978 to an anonymous buyer for a reported $500,000. It is a unique color error (1a****) of Sweden's first stamp, the blue-green three-skilling value of 1857, and was printed in orange when one likeness of it mistakenly appeared on the orange eight-skilling plate. The copy is postally used, and has been owned by several well-known philatelists including Count Ferrari and King Carol of Romania, who sold it in 1950 after his exile. Since the mid-1970s there has been some Swedish opinion that the stamp is a forgery, the opinion being based on alleged paper and color variances, but its authenticity has not as yet (1980) been actually disproved.

France Tete-Beches. Among the best-known European rarities are the several tete-beche pairs of various denominations from France's first stamps, the definitive issue of 1849–50, and the subsequent issue of 1853–60. Tete-beche pairs have one stamp upside down from the other; all of these French tete-beches are highly valuable, a few extremely so as indicated here: 1c**, 2b***, 3c*, 4c**, 6c***, 8b****, 9a***, 15e***, 19a****, 20a**, 21a****. There are a few known blocks from the issues, at least two of which were owned for a time by Maurice Burrus, and an unused block of four of the one-franc lake (21a), which is the rarest item of the group; it was an accidental find and was once in the collection of Theodore Champion.

Japanese Invert. An error from the country's first issue in 1871, the Japanese Invert did not become known until 1973. It is a used five-hundred-mon stamp (4h****) in which the denomination was inverted by mistake and printed in black on a green background, and is the only copy that has come to light from what is believed to have been a sheet of forty. Upon discovery it quickly became one of the several most valuable stamps that vie for second place after the British Guiana Magenta.

Post Office Mauritius. The first two Mauritius stamps, which were issued in 1847 and were the first stamps issued by any British colony, erroneously bore the words POST OFFICE instead of POST PAID. Only five hundred each of the one-penny orange and two-penny dark blue were released (1****, 2****); most are believed to have been used on social invitations by the wife of the island's lieutenant governor, and only about a dozen copies of each are known to exist today. A very few covers exist, one of which has been owned by Arthur Hind and Maurice Burrus. A first day cover is understood to be in the British royal collection, and another is in a collection at the British Museum.

Hawaiian Missionaries. Four Hawaiian rarities (1****, 2**, 3**, 4**), issued in 1851. They earned their nickname from having been used mostly by American missionaries on mail sent home. They are not particularly attractive, being merely an unillustrated typeset design printed in blue, but are among the most famous of the rarities. The scarcest of the four, the two-cent value (1), is alleged to have been the cause of a homicide that occurred in France in 1892 when the owner of a copy of it was murdered apparently so the killer could gain possession of it. The copy was later owned by both Count Ferrari and Maurice Burrus. A Missionaries cover was once owned by Alfred Caspary.

U.S. Postmasters' Provisionals. All of the postmasters' provisionals, which were stamps issued by local postmasters before 1847 when the first government stamps appeared, are rare to some degree. There is only one known copy of two of them, the 1846 five-cent blue issue of Boscawen, New Hampshire (4X1****), and the 1846 five-cent red of Lockport, New York (6X1****). Until 1976 the five-cent blue of Alexandria, Virginia (1X2****), was also believed unique, but in that year a second copy came to light. The Confederate States provisionals of 1861 are considerably less rare overall, but only one copy is known of the five-cent red-brown of Mount Lebanon, Louisiana (60X1**).

Canada Postmaster's Provisional. Only one copy exists of the New Carlisle, Quebec, three-penny black provisional issued in 1851, the first known stamp of the colony of Canada. The unique stamp, which does not appear in all catalogs, rang up a dramatic gain when it was auctioned in London, England, in 1977, realizing double the amount of its auction valuation (****).

U.S. Inverts. The best known of the U.S. inverts is the 1918 twenty-four-cent airmail (C3a****) with a blue airplane upside down in red surround. Only one sheet of one hundred stamps was produced of this rarity; soon after discovery it came into the hands of Colonel Green, who gradually sold it off in blocks and singles. In 1977 one single brought $62,500 at auction. Three inverts appeared in the 1869 regular issue: the fifteen-cent type II brown and blue (119b****) and the twenty-four-cent green and violet (120b***), both with pictorial centers inverted, and the thirty-cent blue and carmine (121b***) with side flags inverted. All are extremely rare, partly because they were from an issue that was unpopular at the time and was replaced within a year. The 1901 Pan-American Exposition issue produced three inverted black pictorial centers, on the one-cent green, two-cent carmine, and four-cent red-brown (294a*, 295a**, 296a*). Fewer than two hundred copies are known of the two-cent variety.

Spain Blue Error. This stamp, although of no particularly interesting background or history, is nevertheless one of the world's most valuable. It is a color error that occurred when an electrotype of the 1851 two-real red stamp of Spain was placed by mistake in the blue six-real plate. Three copies are known of the resultant blue stamp (10a****), one of which is in the British Museum. One of the other two was formerly in the collection of Count Ferrari.

Baden Blue-Green. One of Europe's most valuable rarities, the nine-kreuzer black (4b***) of the 1851 issue of the German state of Baden was printed in error on blue-green paper instead of the correct rose paper. Only a very few copies have survived from the single sheet that was printed. Alfred Caspary and Theodore Champion were two former owners of a copy.

Black Honduras. An airmail stamp of Honduras (C12***), only one copy of which is known to be still in existence although two or three others have reportedly surfaced and then disappeared again. The stamp is one of a quantity of obsolete regular issues of 1915–16 that in 1925 were privately surcharged with government authorization for use with the country's newly introduced airmail service. Three different colors were used for the overprint, the Black's twenty-five-cent surcharge being in black ink on a ten-cent blue stamp. The Black Honduras has been the world's highest-priced airmail issue as well as the most valuable stamp of Central America. At one time it was widely counterfeited, the genuine surcharge having been crudely printed and thus tempting to copy.

Canada Large Queens. Because of the many variations in paper, watermark, color, and perforation, the eight values of the Canadian Large Queens issue of 1868 actually produced around forty cataloged varieties. This resulted in many scarce numbers as well as a few rarities. All of the values were printed on wove paper, and three of the low ones additionally appeared on laid paper. Of the three on laid, only two copies are known of the two-cent green (32***), which is generally recognized as Canada's most expensive single stamp. The watermarked variety on wove paper of the half-cent black (21b*) is next highest in value of the Large Queens, and one of the country's highest overall.

Bavaria Tete-Beche. In the first Bavarian issue in 1849, one stamp was printed upside down on the one-kreuzer black sheet. Three blocks are existent containing this tete-beche (1b***), and they are among Europe's most valuable philatelic items. The best-known block consists of twelve stamps and has been owned by both Count Ferrari and Alfred Lichtenstein.

U.S. Franklin Z-Grill. The rarest U.S. stamp (excluding the few unique postmasters' provisionals) is the one-cent blue of 1867 showing Benjamin Franklin and bearing the Z-pattern grill (85a***). Only two copies are known, one unused and one used; the used is claimed to have realized the highest price at auction of any U.S. stamp. Of the other five Z-grill stamps in the series, two are also rarities: the one-cent green showing Washington (85d**) and the fifteen-cent black showing Lincoln (85f***).

British Guiana Cotton Reel. So called because of its design, a simple unadorned circle containing plain type, this two-cent rose of 1851 was British Guiana's first stamp (1***). With only ten known copies, it ranks high among rarities; six of the copies are in pairs on cover. Count Ferrari owned one of the covers until his death in 1917, after which it was purchased by Maurice Burrus.

Switzerland Double Geneva. The ten-centime double-size black stamp (2L1***) of the Swiss canton of Geneva, issued in 1843 on yellow-green paper and consisting of two identical stamp-size parts that could be used as sold or separated by the mailer to form two five-centime stamps. The Double Genevas are most valuable in their original ten-centime unseparated paired form, especially as vertical pairs, only a few examples of which are known. There is also an extremely valuable block of six that formerly belonged to Maurice Burrus.

Switzerland Rayons. These early Swiss stamps are so called because they bear the word RAYON followed by a Roman numeral. Rayon is French for radius and the number represented the zone, the amount of postage to be paid depending on the distance indicated by the zone number; Rayon I was up to 48 kilometers, Rayon II up to 120 kilometers. The significant Rayons are the 1851 ten-rappen Rayon II (6**) and five-rappen Rayon I (9***), both with colored frame around a central Swiss cross. A ten-rappen Rayon II was among Alfred Caspary's holdings. Issues also appeared without the frame around the cross; they are scarce but not rare. Another early Swiss rarity is the 1850 regular two-and-one-half-rappen without the cross (4**) issued for local use.

Austrian Newspaper. Special-purpose stamps, even if rare, seldom reach top price brackets. An exception is the scarlet six-kreuzer newspaper stamp from the 1851–56 issues of Austria (P4**), which has long been among the world's most valuable stamps. Two other varieties from the same issues, the yellow six-kreuzer (P2*) and the rose thirty-kreuzer (P3**), have also risen to high prices.

Canada Twelve-Pence Chalon. This classic black Canadian stamp (3**) from the country's first issue in 1849 as the Province of Canada shows a portrait of Queen Victoria taken from a well-known painting by Alfred Chalon. The stamp had a short life because of problems deriving from the paper it was printed on, and its denomination, which was for paying a seldom-needed rate, was an additional factor in keeping it from being commonly used for postage. The best-known existent copies are the mint pair acquired by the Canadian National Postal Museum in 1975 and valued at $125,000. They were the subject of the stamp-on-stamp twelve-cent commemorative issued in 1978 (753) to mark the Canadian International Philatelic Exhibition.

Tuscany Provisional. This Tuscan rarity, the ocher three-lira value of 1860 (23**), is not a provisional in the sense of a U.S. provisional, but rather an issue of a provisional government. Several copies are known, and they are usually valued up near the top few stamps of Europe. A few unused and used specimens were in the collection of Alfred Caspary.

U.S. Saint Louis Bears. Eight postmasters' provisionals (11X1*–11X8*) issued in Saint Louis in three denominations between 1845 and 1847, and printed in black on differing colors of paper. They are so called because two rampant bears are the most prominent features of the Missouri coat of arms, which forms the stamps' design. All eight are rare, a twenty-cent variety (11X3**) being the most valuable. The Bears owe much of their fame to two separate chance windfalls, one in Saint Louis in 1895 and the other in Philadelphia in 1912, in which most existing copies were found.

Uruguay Tete-Beches. Tete-beches occurred in two stamps of the 1858 issue of Uruguay, the 120-centesimo blue (4c*) and the 180-centesimo green (5c**). Three tete-beche pairs are known of the former, and two of the latter. In each case one pair is in the British Museum, and Count Ferrari and Alfred Lichtenstein were both former owners of another.

India Queen Victoria Invert. Two copies are known to exist of the India 1854 four-anna issue (6c*) on which the head of Queen Victoria, appearing in red, was inverted on the blue stamp. The error was apparently discovered and corrected quickly. Of the two surviving copies, one is believed to be in the British royal collection. The other was at one time owned by Alfred Caspary; its present whereabouts is not generally known.

The following list is a sampling of the numerous other rarities that are less known and in most cases less valuable. It also is only a representation, picked at random from stamps valued at $5,000 or more.

- Argentina 1862 fifteen-centavo tete-beche pair (7*)
- Bermuda 1848–54 one-penny postmasters (X1***, X2***, X3***)
- Cape of Good Hope 1861 color errors, one-penny (7b*), four-penny (9b**)
- Ceylon 1857 four-penny (5**)
- Great Britain 1882 one-pound (92*)
- Italy 1863 fifteen-centesimo invert (22a*)
- Newfoundland 1860 one-shilling (10**)
- New Zealand 1862 three-penny (15**)
- Romania 1858 twenty-seven-parale tete-beche pair (1a**)
- Russia 1875 seven-kopeck invert (27d**)
- Spain 1854 one-real (33**)

Innumerable stamps that are scarce, but not considered rare, are valued at upwards of one thousand dollars. Most countries except the newest stamp-issuing ones have at least a few high-priced issues, making it generally impractical for an average collector to acquire all the varieties of an individual nation.

Also see Chalons; Confederate States Provisionals; Grill; Invert; Large Queens; Postmasters' Provisionals; Tete-Beche.

149

Redrawn, Reengraved. Both terms refer basically to work performed on the design or engraving of a stamp already in circulation. Such work may be done to alter something specific in the design, or it may be done simply to improve an engraving but end up causing inadvertent minor changes in the design; in either case it usually results in a separate catalog listing for the new stamp. Examples of redrawn and reengraved varieties are common. In the United States there are many from the nineteenth century up through 1922. In Canada there were only a few earlier ones, but several values were redone in the definitive issue introduced in 1967.

Reentry. Occasionally it has happened that when a correction was made in an engraving the original work was not completely erased, resulting in a double image or ghost in the printed stamp. This variation is known as a reentry. It is usually only a curiosity with no particular impact on a stamp's value.

Regionals. Generally speaking, regionals can be any stamps valid for paying postage only from a specified locality or region, but good for delivery inside or outside the region. The U.S. postmasters' provisionals and the Canada Port Hood provisionals are examples of such regional stamps. Specifically, the term is taken to mean the regional stamps of Great Britain first issued in 1958 to be sold only in their identified regions: Scotland, Wales, Northern Ireland, the Isle of Man (until 1971), and the Channel Islands Jersey and Guernsey (both until 1969). Any of the regional stamps can be mailed anywhere in Britain, however; their postal validity is not limited to the areas in which they are sold.

CANADA REGISTERED LETTER ISSUE

U.S. REGISTRY ISSUE

Registered Mail. Special stamps for registered mail have been used by several countries including the United States and Canada. In 1876 Canada issued a Registered Letter set of three values in one design (F1–F3), which with color and perforation varieties totaled six stamps. They were in use until 1889, when it was decided that regular postage stamps could as easily serve to pay registration fees. One or two of them are fairly common used; the others, including all varieties unused, are less common, some being fairly scarce. The United States issued a single Registry stamp in 1911 (F1) that was phased out in favor of regular stamps in 1913. It too is fairly common used, and much less common unused.

Regular Issues. A broad term describing general postage stamps as distinguished from such special-purpose issues as airmail, special delivery, and the like. More specifically it also refers to definitive stamps as distinguished from commemorative and special issues, which are also general postage stamps.

Also see Commemorative; Definitive; Special Issue.

Remainders. At times some countries have sold at a discount to the philatelic wholesale trade quantities of obsolete stamps, the stamps having first been demonetized and sometimes canceled to order. The stamps are called remainders, and the practice—which is considered undesirable by many collectors—remaindering. Neither the United States nor Canada has remaindered any issues.

Also see Canceled to Order; Demonetization.

Removing Paper from Stamps. When separating stamps from pieces of cover or other adhering paper you should always remove the paper from the stamp, as the title of this article indicates, not the stamp from the paper. What this means in practice is that when a stamp doesn't float completely free of paper and needs an assist, it's the paper you should peel away; by doing so you minimize the risk of tearing or thinning the stamp.

Not every stamp should be separated from a full cover. While modern covers including the commonplace first day ones are seldom worth preserving, there is a chance that an earlier stamp on cover should be left as it is; sometimes the postmarks and other evidence of postal use are of more value than the stamp.

It is usually necessary or desirable, however, to free stamps from any adhering paper pieces including old hinge remnants. Stamps to be freed can be divided roughly into three groups requiring different methods: stamps that can safely be soaked (the overwhelming majority), stamps that should not be soaked, and stamps stuck to other stamps.

Stamps That Can Be Soaked. This group includes almost everything from present-day mail with these few possible exceptions: The colors run on some brightly hued envelopes and can permanently stain stamps; colors can also run on photogravure stamps, which are identified as such in their catalog listings, and on stamps printed with aniline or other fugitive inks; and parts of the paper surface, and with it the design, can wash away on stamps printed on chalky paper. In most of these cases the danger of harm is not great, but some individual experimenting is wise before soaking stamps in any of the questionable categories.

The easiest way to free soakable stamps is to drop a batch of them into a few inches of lukewarm water in a sink, stir them loose so all surfaces are being wetted, and let them soak for fifteen to twenty minutes. By that time most should have sunk clear of their paper, or at least the paper should be easy to peel away. Occasionally the gum on certain foreign stamps has longer cling, but release can be hastened by adding a few drops of detergent to the water. Some gums leave an undesirable trace after the paper comes away; this residue can be felt and removed by light rubbing with a finger. To prevent damage to wet stamps it is best to handle them without tongs, with particular care taken with pairs and blocks to avoid perforation tear.

Next lay the wet stamps between thick towels to remove excess water, then press-dry by placing them carefully flat in a drying book or—less expensive and just as good—between blotting pads weighted down with a telephone directory or other large heavy book. Blotting pads can be made from a desk blotter cut to convenient-size sheets, or can consist of nothing more than the pulpy backing cardboards from padded stationery. Press-drying takes a few hours or overnight and leaves flat specimens free of water-induced wrinkles. Stamps should never be mounted in an album until they are perfectly dry; damp stamps can cause a permanent pucker in the page.

Stamps That Should Not Be Soaked. This group includes stamps bearing colored cancellations, some precanceled stamps, and the questionable categories mentioned above. One separation method is to float such stamps right side up on lukewarm water until the gum softens enough for the paper to be peelable without damage to the stamp; the face of the stamp can be kept dry if this is done carefully. Another method is to place the stamps in a humidifier until the same result is achieved.

Both of these methods leave much of the gum still on the stamp and also encourage curling. In press-drying these stamps, therefore, their gum side should be placed on glass or hard plastic instead of on a blotting pad; they will not stick tight to either of these surfaces when dry. They may end up with a slight curl, but this usually rights itself a while after they have been held flat in an album or stock book.

Stamps Stuck to Other Stamps. These are almost invariably mint stamps stored without proper precaution under humid conditions (and perhaps stuck to something else besides other stamps). The only practical way to separate them is with a humidifier, after which they are bound to be left with some degree of gum damage. They also must be press-dried on glass or plastic and are subject to the curling that eventually rights itself after they are mounted. The best cure for mint stamps stuck to other stamps is prevention of the condition in the first place by taking the precautions given in the article on storing stamps.

Also see Humidifier; Storing Stamps.

Renovating Soiled or Damaged Stamps. Doctoring stamps to increase their value constitutes fakery, but there is nothing wrong with improving the appearance of stamps that are dirty, pencil-marked, creased, torn, or variously stained. The following simple ways to treat such defects should in many cases be attempted only on inexpensive stamps. Judgment is involved here; with some of the treatments you have to take the stamp's value into account, and whether possible additional damage would be worse than its untreated condition. Treatment to valuable stamps should be applied extremely carefully, or very often not at all. Stamps printed by photogravure, with fugitive inks, or on chalky paper should be subjected to water only with caution. A few of the methods shown require following with press-drying, which is described in the article on removing paper from stamps.

Dirt. Rub a dirty stamp with a finger moistened with ordinary hand soap, rubbing outwards so as not to damage the perforation teeth, and lightly to avoid paper or design damage. Rinse the stamp in water, then press-dry.

Pencil Marks. A soft eraser should clean up pencil and other nonpermanent marks. To contain the erasure and prevent tearing, erase through a typist's shield. If the mark is stubborn let it stay rather than overwork it and risk rubbing away some of the design.

Creases. Soak the stamp in warm water until the paper is fully softened, then press-dry. Unless the paper fibers are broken, this should make the crease disappear.

Tears. After accurately lining up the torn edges on the front of the stamp, apply a piece of hinge to the back. Cut the piece only big enough to cover the tear, and to avoid pucker do not overmoisten it when applying.

Grease. Treatments for grease and oil stains are comparatively drastic and should be given extra forethought and care. One method is to swish the stamp in boiling water for repeated periods of a few seconds; often this will dissolve grease, but note that it may cause some reds and many nineteenth-century blues and violets to fade in color. Another method is to lay the stamp in paint solvent in a shallow tray until the stain disappears. But watch the process closely and discontinue it if the stamp's design or the postmark starts to be affected; some inks are vulnerable to such solvents.

Paraffin Wax. Place the stamp between blotters and press it with a hot iron, which may cause the wax to migrate from the stamp into the blotting paper. This method also works for some grease residues.

Mildew. This usually shows as spots on stamps, and is especially prevalent on stamps in tropical climates. Try painting the spot with a solution of household bleach. Start with a very weak solution—a couple of drops of bleach in a tablespoon of water—increasing the strength as needed until the effective point is reached. Then wash the stamp with water and press-dry.

Oxidization (Rust). This shows as a darkening of color; it is common on old orange and red-brown stamps of many countries including the United States. To restore brightness, paint such stamps with hydrogen peroxide, wash the peroxide off with water when the proper color has returned, and press-dry the stamp.

Fading. Try the hydrogen peroxide treatment described for oxidization; it may help, but true fading is permanent and cannot really be corrected. Sometimes apparent fading is nothing more than dirt, and can be treated as such.

Also see Removing Paper from Stamps.

Replica. A reproduction of a stamp made to size and printed in a single color, meant for filling an album space otherwise likely to remain empty. Most replicas were of the scarcer early stamps and produced in the nineteenth century, when they were fairly common as space fillers. They were not issued for any fraudulent purpose, usually being enough different from the stamps to be readily recognized as copies;

but sometimes a particularly true replica was mistakenly branded a forgery. Because of this potential for deceit, replicas were disapproved of by many countries and eventually their production was mostly discontinued.

Also see Facsimile.

Rep Paper, Repp Paper. See Paper Types and How to Distinguish Them.

Reprints. This term is best limited in meaning to authorized reprintings from original plates of discontinued stamps, which have occasionally been produced by many countries for official records, files, or souvenirs, with no intention of actually reissuing the stamps. Additional printings of stamps still in circulation are not truly reprints, although sometimes so called.

Revenue Stamp. A stamp designed for use in paying excise tax or other government levy for stock transfer, customs duty, document registration, license, or other legal or official business. Countries using revenue stamps include the United States and Canada. Some countries at times have used postage stamps as revenues, or revenue stamps for postage. In Great Britain all stamps serve both purposes, accounting for the inscription POSTAGE-REVENUE that appeared on most Great Britain definitives and a few commemoratives from 1880 until the 1960s. This practice is also followed in some British Commonwealth and other countries.

U.S. EXPRESS REVENUE

Ribbed Paper. See Paper Types and How to Distinguish Them.

Roll Stamps. See Coil Stamps.

Rotary Press. See Printing Methods and How to Distinguish Them.

Rotogravure. See Printing Methods and How to Distinguish Them.

Rouletting. A form of perforating consisting of slits in the paper, not holes, and with no paper removed. There are several rouletting patterns, all derived from straight lines, vees, or curves. Rouletting was a common method of separation in the nineteenth century but is little used today except for special purposes, as in the 1967 Chagall souvenir sheet (179) of the United Nations. This entire sheet was devoted to a stained-glass memorial window, but it could be separated into six individual stamps; for aesthetic reasons rouletting was used for the separations, since it is not readily noticeable and therefore less likely to detract from the design as long as the sheet is left intact. For the same reason, some collectors feel that rouletting should have been used on the U.S. multistamp single scenes of the bicentennial years (1480–1483, 1629–1631, 1691–1694).

Also see Perforation.

Routing Stickers. Self-adhesive labels used since 1975 by the U.S. Postal Service and bulk mailers to simplify mail handling. There are five different routing stickers, each bearing a bold single letter or numeral in black on a brightly colored background. A sticker is placed on the top piece of a sorted bundle to indicate how much forwarding the entire bundle can receive before needing further sorting. This allows it to be sent unbroken to the proper distribution facility: state, sectional, city primary, or city secondary. The code is as follows:

S on orange: All pieces are for the same state.

3 on green: All pieces carry the same first three Zip Code digits, but are for different towns.

C on yellow: All pieces carry the same first three Zip Code digits, and are for the same city.

D on red: All pieces carry the same complete five-digit Zip Code.

F on blue: All pieces are for the same addressee.

Row. For convenience in locating stamps on a sheet, row usually means horizontal, and column, vertical.

Rust on Stamps. See Renovating Soiled and Damaged Stamps.

Saint Lawrence Seaway. This international inland navigation system, extending 2,342 miles from the western end of the Great Lakes to the Atlantic Ocean, was the subject of the first identically designed U.S. and Canadian stamps. The seaway was dedicated by President Eisenhower and Queen Elizabeth II on June 26, 1959, and on the same day commemorated with a four-cent value in the United States (1131) and a five-cent value in Canada (387). Some copies of the Canadian stamp were discovered with an inverted center (387a), a scarce and valuable error.

Saint Louis Bears. Popular name for eight U.S. postmasters' provisionals (11X1–11X8) issued in Saint Louis in 1845–47 and showing the Missouri coat of arms, which prominently features two rampant bears. All eight are rarities.

Also see Rarities: U.S. Saint Louis Bears.

Sales Circuit. A system for buying and selling stamps within a closed group, usually simply called a circuit (see).

Schermack Perforation. In 1906 several U.S. makers of vending machines began applying their own perforations to unperforated four-hundred-stamp sheets. The perforations, which appeared only on low values, were in various styles designed for the manufacturer's own machines, and were in use by one company—Schermack—as late as the 1922 definitive series. The Schermack Type III perforation, easily identified by its two straight-edged oblong holes instead of a series of round ones, is by far the most common of all private perforations; it was introduced after the original Schermack Company, of Detroit, had become the Mailometer Company. Other vending-machine companies with their own perforations were Brinkerhoff, Farwell, International Vending Machine, and U.S. Automatic Vending. Stamps bearing any of these commercial perforations are generally priced lower than their regularly perforated counterparts.

Scott. The worldwide stamp catalogs most widely used in the United States and Canada, published annually in several volumes by the Scott Publishing Co. In both countries Scott catalog numbers are the generally recognized means of identifying stamps. As the publisher is not also a dealer offering stamps for sale at the prices shown, some collectors feel that Scott prices are not true market values; nevertheless they are usually accepted as the basis for setting prices, especially for common stamps.

Also see Catalog; Catalog Value.

se. Straight edge (see).

Secret Marks. Most so-called secret marks on stamps are not secret at all, but for identification purposes. Thus the best-known marks, those on the U.S. issue of 1873 which was produced by the Continental Bank Note Company (156–166), were placed on the stamps to distinguish them from the previous issues of identical design printed by the National Bank Note Company. There are countless other examples of secret marks, which have appeared on the stamps of Great

Britain, Japan, and China, among other countries. Other examples of identifying marks are the tiny year dates on many stamps of Canada. Some of the stamps on which the date can readily be seen under a magnifying glass are the 1935 ten-cent value showing a mounted policeman (223), the 1937 four-cent Citizenship issue (275), and the 1961 five-cent Resources for Tomorrow issue (395); the two eight-cent Canadian Churchmen stamps of 1975 (662–663) carry a copyright notice as well as the date.

Seebeck Issues. In the late nineteenth century Nicholas F. Seebeck and the Hamilton Bank Note Company of New York contracted to supply certain Central and South American countries with their postage stamps free of charge, in return for which the countries would discontinue and demonetize the issues regularly and the suppliers would be allowed to use the plates to print additional quantities of the stamp for sale to collectors. The issues so affected were those of Ecuador 1894–96, Honduras 1896, Nicaragua 1896–98, and Salvador 1891–98; some postage dues and officials were also produced under the agreement. The additional quantities printed are mostly distinguishable by differences in paper, and are of little value. The Seebeck issues have always been held in disrepute, and in addition they caused the countries involved to lose favor among collectors for many years.

Selling a Stamp Collection. Almost every stamp collection of value will some day be offered for sale, if not by the collector himself then by his estate. When that eventuality arrives it is almost a certainty that unless the collection includes some properties that have significantly increased in value since they were acquired, it will not realize what the owner might feel it is worth, or even pay back just the money invested in it. The main reason for this is that a collection must be sold at wholesale, though for the most part it is acquired at retail. But stamp collecting is first of all a pleasure-giving hobby, so it's perfectly reasonable that it should carry a cost like any other hobby; generally, any profit it might produce should be treated as a bonus windfall, not as a rightful return. And as in selling anything else, there are ways to help obtain the most favorable buying offer; among other things it is important to tender the collection to the proper market, and to make sure the collection is showcased to its best advantage. You should also have a realistic idea of how much you hope to get for it, as you'll have to set an asking price or if it's to be appraised you'll need a guideline for knowing if you're satisfied with the appraisal; see Inventorying a Stamp Collection for suggestions on arriving at a dollar value.

Where to Sell. Local dealers are always potential buyers for an average collection worth up to a few hundred dollars. Sometimes there's an advantage in going to a dealer you've done business with over the years; otherwise for the best chance of a good offer start with a large active dealer who can anticipate quick turnover. Normally dealers buy outright for cash most collections up to medium size, giving you the benefit of immediate payment; the bigger the dealer, the bigger the collection he can handle. Another arrangement is to consign the collection to the dealer for him to sell by what is known as private treaty, which means that he will try to find a buyer at the price you have set or a negotiated compromise, paying you minus prearranged commission after the sale has been made. The disadvantages of this method are that it may take a long time, and that it usually works only for small collections of low value, the kind a grandfather might buy as a starter for a grandson; for the reasons noted below, collectors seldom buy complete collections. In choosing a dealer try to avoid the middleman type, one who in turn will sell the material to other dealers. Instead go to a dealer who sells exclusively to collectors, because he sells at retail and can afford to pay more than one who resells at wholesale.

If your collection is particularly valuable, or if it is strong in specialized material, you will have to find a large dealer, possibly one who conducts periodic mail sales or auctions. Again, you can usually choose between outright immediate sale and consignment. At this level consignment will most likely be for inclusion of the material in the dealer's sale or auction, for which the collection will be broken up and lotted into sets or individual stamps. One of the reasons for choosing consignment over outright sale is that in the long run it may realize more money even after the dealer's commission (twenty percent is fairly standard) is deducted. Against this is the longer time it takes, and the fact that payment is piecemeal as lots are offered and sold. Most large out-of-town dealers and auction houses can arrange to receive material by mail, and some will send a buying representative for a major collection; their ads appear regularly in philatelic periodicals. For the specialized collection try to work with a dealer who is strong in the same specialty, whether it's a country, an era, or items like covers or nonpostal stamps.

It is widely assumed—sometimes even stated in stamp columns and literature—that other stamp collectors are likely buyers for a collection. This is rarely true, for at least three reasons. The first is a matter of money—few except wealthy collectors can afford to buy at one time much more than a low-value collection. The second is that much of the purchase price would simply go toward buying duplicates of the collector's present holdings. The most significant reason, however, is the fact that the pleasure in stamp collecting lies in the chase—in the gradual acquisition of elusive numbers, not in securing an instant collection—as your own collecting philosophy will undoubtedly confirm.

Appraisals. Any dealer offer to buy a collection must be preceded by an appraisal of it. For packet-material collections of little value the appraisal will be hardly more than the dealer flipping through the album pages, but collections of any consequence require detailed calculation. An appraisal is a professional piece of work and must be paid for, the fee usually being a percentage of total arrived-at value. In actual practice a dealer's appraisal is also his offer to buy, and the fee is generally waived if the buying offer is accepted; but appraisals for a fee can also be had independently, with no buying offer involved (for tax purposes, for instance). Instead of a value percentage, an appraisal fee can be based on the number of stamps in the collection, an arrangement many feel is preferable.

Selling Tips. It is well recognized that to be accorded a high reasonable appraised value a collection must be shown to best advantage. Proper organization, careful attention to appearance, and elimination of minus factors can when taken together increase a collection's appraisal by as much as fifty percent, according to many experts. Following are some of the recommended ways to accomplish this.

1. Do not break the collection and offer it in segments. The more complete a holding is, the higher its total realization will be.

2. Do not remove valuable items for separate disposition. Their presence will make the whole collection more desirable and probably induce an appraisal higher than the total

they and the balance of the stamps would bring separately. In addition, some dealers aren't interested at all in a depleted album, and anyone with experience can tell quickly if he is looking at nothing but packet material.

3. Take care that no stamps are misidentified—for example, an unwatermarked stamp mounted in the space for an identical but watermarked one. Misidentification will cause the dealer to assume that with same-face varieties the one in the space is the cheapest one. He will also deduct for the time he'll expect to spend later in checking varieties before selling them.

4. Remove such obvious seconds and defective stamps as those with obliterating postmarks and pieces torn away. Not only do they spoil the appearance, but they have a downgrading effect on the entire collection.

5. Call attention by means of a note on the page to any superb or very fine earlier stamps that might be in the collection, as these are usually valued at well over catalog (see Condition).

6. Be sure the album looks well kept, mounting is neat and straight, and mint stamps are not spot-stuck to pages. The first two are important psychologically, the last has a direct bearing on value.

Selvage. The unprinted edges on a pane of stamps, separated from the stamps by perforation. The margin, that part of the pane on which the plate numbers and postal slogans appear, is selvage.

Semipostal. A stamp bearing a small surtax in addition to its postage value, the tax going to a specified charity or other cause. The first semipostals were issued in New South Wales in 1897 (B1–B2) in aid of the colony's home for consumptives. The best known are the Switzerland Pro Juventute series, issued annually (except 1914) since 1913, with the surtax used to help fund work among the country's youth. There are no U.S. semipostals, but between 1974 and 1976 Canada issued twelve of them (B1–B12) to help underwrite the Olympic Games held in Montreal in 1976.

Sesquicentennial. A one-hundred-fiftieth anniversary, sometimes noted with a commemorative stamp. Typical sesquicentennial emissions include the U.S. 1939 Washington Inauguration commemorative (854) and the Canada 1934

BELGIUM SEMIPOSTAL

New Brunswick commemorative (210); both countries have issued others besides.

Se-Tenant. A French phrase meaning holding together, or holding to itself. The term can refer broadly to any stamps not separated from each other, but in practice is limited to describing stamps of differing design printed next to each other on the same pane, usually in blocks of two, three, or four. Se-tenant blocks lose much of their value when separated. This is especially true of used blocks, where a single stamp would in most cases have been enough to pay postage and canceled blocks are therefore scarce and likely to have been canceled to order; an exception is in the U.S. 1972 National Parks Centennial issue, the block of four two-cent stamps (1448–1451), all of which were needed to pay the eight-cent first-class mail rate of the time. The first U.S. se-tenant issue was the block of four Christmas stamps in 1964 (1254–1257), and the concept has since become commonly used, with at least one se-tenant pair or block every year since 1967. Canada's first se-tenant was the 1957 Outdoor Recreation issue block of four (365–368); others have been issued occasionally, including one six-variety set, the Centenary of Letter Carrier Delivery issue in 1974 (634–639).

Set. All of the stamps of a single definitive or commemorative issue. Generally the term means three or more stamps, not merely a pair.

Sheet. Strictly, the form in which stamps come off the printing press, typically containing four panes separated by gutters. The sheet is cut to make the panes, the form in which the stamps are sold at the post office. The panes themselves are popularly called sheets, and although technically it is incorrect to do so, there is actually little real reason for preserving the distinction. The term also refers to commemorative souvenir or miniature sheets of one or more stamps.

Silk Paper. See Paper Types and How to Distinguish Them.

Silver Jubilee. A celebration marking a twenty-fifth anniversary; in philately the term usually refers to the twenty-fifth anniversary of the accession of a British sovereign. There have been two such in this century, both marked by jubilee issues in many British Commonwealth countries. In Canada George V's Silver Jubilee in 1935 was commemorated with a six-stamp set (211–216) and Elizabeth II's in 1977 with a single stamp (704).

Also see Jubilee.

Slogan. Slogans are used philatelically in two different environments apart from postage-meter impressions. One is on the margins of stamp panes, the phrases like USE ZIP CODE and others. The second is as part of postmarks, in which the slogan may be a postal instruction as on pane margins, or a seasonal or charity message. Both margin and postmark slogans are sometimes collected as specialties.

Small Queens. Popular name for the Canada Queen Victoria issues of 1870 and later (34–45), which remained in use until 1897. They consisted of eight values from half-cent to fifteen cents, all bearing a profile portrait of the queen. They are about an eighth-inch smaller both ways than the so-called Large Queens, which they replaced in the interest of paper and production economies. The Small Queens have consistently been among Canada's favorite issues with collectors, for several reasons. One is that most values are still available in ample quantities, particularly used, because of the length of time the issues were current; in addition there are varieties in printing and perforation, and many minor varieties in color shadings, to interest the specialist or variety hunter.

Also see Large Queens.

Socked on the Nose. Colloquialism describing a postmark perfectly centered on the stamp. For suggested positioning of the stamp to help obtain this desirable cancellation hit, see Bull's-Eye.

Souvenir Card. A picture card that may or may not be of mailing size, to which a stamp is affixed and then postmarked often on the first day of issue. The card is selected for its illustration, which should have some relationship to the stamp's theme. Souvenir cards, purely an avocation of some collectors, have no philatelic value.

Souvenir Sheet. A postal sheet embracing one or more stamps, usually a commemorative or promotional emission. In most cases it consists of the stamp or stamps printed imperforate and surrounded by wide margins bearing an inscription. The sheet in its entirety is valid for postage (but often impractical because of its size) as are its individual stamps, which may be identical to an issue in concurrent use. However, souvenir sheets are really just that—souvenirs, a means of producing revenue; they are never postally necessary, and no collector should feel any need to buy them. Noteworthy U.S. examples of unnecessary souvenir sheets were the four Bicentennial ones of 1976 (1686–1689), each consisting of a revolution-era color scene about six by four inches with five commemorative stamps perforated into it; the sheets were considered obvious excesses by collectors generally, and have never attained any real popularity. Other U.S. souvenir sheets have appeared infrequently. Canada's first was issued in 1978 to mark CAPEX, the Canadian International Philatelic Exhibition (766a).

In most foreign countries souvenir sheets are called miniature sheets, and the term souvenir sheet usually refers to a sheet showing something of philatelic interest but no postal validity. In the United States and Canada the terms are interchangeable.

Sower, the. One of the world's best-known stamp designs, a classical figure broadcasting seed, used on definitive stamps of France from 1903 until 1938 (138–184). The design appeared with two different backgrounds and was issued in many denominations, colors, and minor varieties over its long life.

Space Filler. A badly defective stamp, of use only to fill an album space until a better copy can be obtained or if one is unobtainable. Space fillers are almost worthless, except in the case of stamps so scarce as to give any available copy some degree of value. There is mixed opinion on carrying space fillers in a collection; many collectors feel that a blank space is preferable. In any event space fillers should be removed from the album pages of a collection about to be appraised or sold, as they add no value and tend to downgrade the collection overall.

Spandrel. This architectural term, which describes the triangular space formed by the outside curve of an arch and the inside corner of its surrounding framework, is used philatelically to describe similar triangles, either top or bottom, formed between a circle or oval around a stamp design and the surrounding rectangular frame. Spandrels in the first U.S. issues in 1847 (1–2) contained the country initials at the top and the denomination figure or letter at the

EDWARD VII SPANDRELS

164

bottom. More clearly defined examples are in the 1903 King Edward VII issue of Canada (89–95), in which each denomination carries a crown in the top spandrels and the denomination numeral in the bottom.

Special Delivery. Special delivery does not mean expedited forwarding between cities or post offices, but rather immediate delivery to the addressee when the piece arrives at the destination post office. In the United States special-delivery stamps were introduced in 1885; most of the twenty-three varieties issued through 1971 (E1–E23) are common or fairly so, there being a few scarcities in some of the early numbers unused. Canada's first special-delivery stamp appeared in 1898 and the last in 1946, after which the series was discontinued in favor of regular postage stamps; none of the eleven varieties issued (E1–E11) are particularly scarce.

Special Handling. This postal service is designed to provide, for an extra charge, expeditious handling of parcels. In the United States in 1925 five special-handling stamps were issued in four denominations and a color variety (QE1–QE4a) and remained in use for several years until they were discontinued in favor of regular postage stamps; all are fairly common. There have been no Canadian special-handling stamps.

Specialization. There is nothing wrong with the beginning stamp collector hoarding everything that comes his way— such generalization is desirable at first, as it provides him with a basic philatelic education and a taste of all the fields in his chosen hobby. But no one can give even passing attention to more than a fraction of the 200,000 existing stamps and the flood of thousands of new ones each year. So every collector except the confirmed dilettante soon reaches a point where he has to limit his collecting interests by selecting areas of specialization.

It should be pointed out that specialization strictly means something quite different from limitation; the collector who limits himself to a single country, for example, is not necessarily a specialist in the country. A true specialist does more than just collect his specialty, which may even be one single stamp. If it is he collects it on covers, in proofs, and in other available forms; he looks for undiscovered minor varieties of it; he studies its postal history; sometimes he contributes to its literature by publishing new data on it.

U.S. SPECIAL DELIVERY ISSUE

CANADA SPECIAL DELIVERY ISSUE

(Stanley B. Ashbrook, who died in 1958 at seventy-six, spent most of his philatelic lifetime on a single stamp, the U.S. one-cent blue Franklin of 1851–56 (5–9) and 1857–61 (18–24). The stamp was issued in thirteen major varieties and at least as many minor ones; none are common, some are very scarce, and one (5) is a rarity. Ashbrook wrote two books and other published works on the stamp.) A true specialist, obviously, is an advanced collector. But since specialization is a term generally accepted to describe what is actually only limitation, as used here it mostly means only limitation.

The following general areas of specialization are listed as starting suggestions for the collector who has decided to restrict his interests or add a new interest to his present ones.

A Country or Countries. Collecting only a chosen country or group of countries is the most prevalent way to specialize. It is a natural step away from collecting everything because the omnicollector almost inevitably finds himself partial to particular countries, and it is popular enough that there is at least one collectors' club or society devoted to just about every philatelically important country. When groups of countries are collected they may be linked geographically, like the nations of South America, or politically, like the British Commonwealth—or they may have nothing in common at all except the collector's interest in them. An overwhelming majority of collectors appear to collect the stamps of their own country whether or not they collect anything else. A survey made in 1978 among members of an international philatelic organization showed 88 percent of American members collecting U.S. stamps, with almost half of them collecting U.S. exclusively; an even higher number of Canadians—92 percent—collected Canadian stamps, although only about a sixth of them did so exclusively.

Time Periods. Collecting by time periods can mean, for example, collecting only the stamps of the nineteenth century, which by definition is generally challenging and expensive. Or it can mean any other time period that appeals to the collector: the whole twentieth century, or parts of it like pre-World War I, between the wars (1919–38), or post-World War II. In British Commonwealth countries time periods often follow years of reigns, common segments being Victoria, the Edwards and Georges, and Elizabeth; the last-named period is popular enough to warrant the specialized Elizabethan Commonwealth catalog published annually since 1965 by the Stanley Gibbons firm of London. Since collections limited by country or time period are thus also limited in numbers of admissible stamps, they are often fleshed out with minor varieties and pertinent collateral material.

Selected Issues. Typical selected issues might be the Europa series released in concert annually since 1956 by cooperating European nations now numbering a majority of those on the continent; for reasons considered detrimental to philately these issues at one time suffered temporary loss of repute, but remain nevertheless an interesting way to specialize on a multicountry basis (see Europa). Other issues for specialization, at random: the Germania series of Germany 1900–1921, the Kangaroo series of Australia 1913–45, or the Sower series of France 1903–38 (see Germania, Kangaroos, Sower); the Pro Juventute (see) annual semipostals of Switzerland; the prerevolutionary stamps of Russia of which there are well over one hundred, most of them fairly common. A favorite single stamp for intensive collecting is the 1864 one-penny rose-red of Great Britain, which was issued with 150-odd plate numbers, the numbers being visible under a glass in the scroll framework of the stamp's design; these plate varieties were issued in large quantities and with only a few exceptions are available at low prices. Other issues with built-in limitations are the three-cent commemoratives of the United States, which consist of around two hundred stamps issued between 1932 and 1958; and similarly, the five-cent commemoratives of Canada, of which almost one hundred were issued between 1954 and 1968. Issues that are relatively easy to obtain and perhaps even complete (for instance the U.S. and Canadian commemoratives mentioned) can be made more challenging by being collected in several ways: used, mint, mint blocks, and on cover, to name a few possibilities.

Special-Purpose Stamps. Collecting airmails, perhaps all the airmails of the world, is one example of special-purpose specialization; or instead of airmails the collection could be of any of the several other separately cataloged special-purpose emissions. Official stamps, which have been issued by many countries and are to some extent neglected by generalists, are among the most popular issues for special-purpose collectors.

Topical Stamps. Collecting stamps by subject matter without regard to country, era, or other defined limits is a wide and popular field that is really not specialization at all, but a branch of philately with its own internal specialization by subject. It is more fully described under Topical Collecting (see).

Other Philatelic Material. Many collectors specialize in such collateral material as covers, cut squares, postage-meter imprints, postal stationery, or precancels, to give just a sampling; each of these is defined and described under its own heading in this book.

Special-Purpose Stamps. Stamps designed to pay for postal services other than regular mail. Airmail, special delivery, postage due, and official business are some of the functions handled with special-purpose stamps.

Special Stamp. A stamp classed somewhere between a definitive and a commemorative, and serving to publicize a particular program or cause. Special stamps have shorter life than definitives, usually, but longer than commemoratives. The two U.S. stamps issued in 1977 to promote energy conservation and development (1723–1724) are special stamps.

Specimen. A stamp invalidated for postage by being overprinted or perforated with the word SPECIMEN (or its counterpart on a foreign-language stamp). Specimens are generally copies of new issues produced for archives or other domestic purposes, or for distribution to other countries for identification needs. They sometimes appear on the philatelic market, where there is no complete agreement on whether or not they are legitimately collectible as postage stamps.

de Sperati, Jean (1883–1957). A prolific French forger of stamps, who in 1952 in Paris was fined, assessed heavy damages, and sentenced to imprisonment. His workmanship was good enough that most of his voluminous forgeries are barely detectable, and at least one book has been published cataloging his output. Altogether there were Sperati forgeries for almost one hundred countries, and although the number of different ones per country was usually under ten, there were many more in some cases; the countries most affected were France with eighty-nine Speratis, Spain with eighty, and Switzerland with seventy-three.

There were a few U.S. and Confederate States Speratis, but no Canadian.

Stamps as Investments. The fact that stamps can be valuable assets is continually being demonstrated by announced realizations for auctions and private-treaty sales. And although exact figures are seldom available for complete collections, especially vast ones which must be broken up and liquidated over numerous sales, it's safe to say that among the famous collections sold during this century both the Ferrari and Hind ones brought well over $1 million, the former after World War I and the latter during the depression, and in the 1950s the Caspary collection realized closer to $3 million. It's probably also safe to say that these (like similar large holdings) were sold for more than they cost, even though their costs cannot be determined; but what is different about them compared to an average collection is that they included numerous items only a millionaire could afford in the first place, the kinds of rarities that almost automatically go up in price every time they change hands. Guaranteed profit like that extends only occasionally to the average kinds of stamps found in average collections.

The investment-minded collector must also remember a basic philatelic fact of life: He will almost never sell stamps to another collector at the going retail price, which is what he usually originally paid himself; he will sell instead to a dealer at wholesale—often below half of retail—or through a dealer minus a commission that could be twenty percent of realized value (see Selling a Stamp Collection). What this means is that a stamp must increase in value by an amount equal to the eventual selling discount for him to just break even. This does happen many times, often by amounts big enough to show the seller substantial profits. The reality is that there are overwhelmingly more times when it doesn't happen. Just as with Wall Street stocks, there are no sure things.

If you feel you want to buy stamps for investment despite these facts, the best general rule is to look for comparatively expensive items with a record of steady price increases from year to year. Historically, such items are the ones most likely to continue appreciating in value, and they're usually at price levels where increases can be high enough to leave a net profit after selling expenses. The same amount of money invested in a host of cheaper stamps doesn't have the same

169

chance of growing; price increases in such stamps, even if they do come about, are seldom enough to net a profit. Yet this rule is not infallible; exceptions have disproved it many times in the past, and will certainly do so in the future. It's the rule that overall seems to offer the most reasonable chance for profit, that's all.

Another fair generalization is that you can seldom turn a profit on today's new issues. The habit followed by countless thousands of U.S. and Canadian collectors of laying in their country's commemoratives as they come out serves only to tie up money with little hope of gain. This is because generally the quantities printed are so staggering, with millions of them bought and held by collectors, that the stamps will never become scarce. The situation is often demonstrated by the stamps used on a dealer's mail. If his postage is made up with several commemoratives some-times twenty or thirty years old, they probably came from one of two sources: Either he is using up some of his stocks that have little market demand, or he has bought at a discount from face value the investment stamps of a col-lector who has given up on them. It makes little difference whether you hold blocks, full mint panes, or first day covers—there are just too many of them around. And the same thing is largely true for all stamp-issuing countries.

If you're an average collector of ordinary means consider-ing stamps as an investment, you have to think in terms of buying at retail the lower-priced items that usually promise only minor appreciation, and selling later at wholesale—a proposition much less attractive than putting the money in a savings account where even at six percent interest it will double itself if you leave it for twelve years. The average collector is well advised to enjoy his hobby as a hobby without expecting it to be also a profitable venture.

State Flags Issue. A controversial U.S. issue of 1976, with a different state flag on each of the fifty thirteen-cent stamps on a full single pane (1633–1682). The issue drew wide criticism from collectors and stamp societies and was boycotted by many who considered it purely a revenue-producing emission designed to sell hobbyists fifty postally superfluous stamps. Nevertheless it quickly became in demand and commercially successful, with both mint panes and used single copies bringing almost double their face value within a year.

Stock Book, Stock Card. A stock book is an album-size book with around a dozen shallow pockets running the width of each page, the pages being of lightweight cardboard and the pockets of cardboard, binder's cloth, or transparent plastic and serving as a convenient place for storing and protecting unmounted stamps. Stock books are used by collectors to hold newly acquired stamps before they are permanently mounted, as well as to hold duplicates. Dealers use them to hold stamps for sale, usually books with cardboard pockets on which price information can be marked for each stamp. Pocket-size books of a few pages are also available and are handy for carrying new purchases or duplicates for trading. Stock cards are similar to stock-book pages, generally measuring about four by six inches with three or four pockets; they are mostly used by dealers for mailing approvals or ordered stamps.

Storing Stamps. The silent enemies of stamp condition are excessive dryness, excessive humidity, strong direct light, and lack of air circulation, the last-named tending to intensify the effects of dryness or humidity. Some stamps resist damaging atmospheric conditions better than others, depending mostly on the type of paper used for them, but all are vulnerable to some degree.

Excessive dryness over long periods of time makes a stamp brittle, occasionally even to the point of cracking; it can also harm the gum on mint stamps by causing it to check. Except in unusual circumstances drying out can be prevented by simple precautions. The most obvious one is to avoid storing stamps too close to sources of heat. Also they should not be sealed off from air, which supplies them with the little moisture they actually need. This means that it's best to store albums and stock books upright rather than lay them on top of each other with the pages pressed together. Used stamps kept in glassine envelopes receive enough air as long as the envelope is not packed tight.

Humidity is less damaging than dryness to used stamps, but much more so to mint stamps with gum. Besides making gummed stamps curl it causes them to stick to each other, or to album pages, or to the insides of glassines or other means of storing. Under some conditions it can cause sticking very quickly, even in a matter of days; thus it's important in areas of high humidity to take preventive measures soon after acquiring mint stamps, and to check them regularly for possible harm. Simple preventives include keeping the gummed sides of the stamps dusted with talcum powder. A further step, especially for full panes, is to store them in a closed container—a plastic box big enough to hold panes flat is ideal—with silica gel or other desiccant; but note that the stamps should be removed regularly for airing. Air circulation is even more important for gummed stamps than it is for used, and mint copies stored in anything including glassine envelopes should be periodically allowed to air for a few hours, most particularly in high-humidity regions. (Some collectors in tropical climates recommend laying albums of mint stamps flat so the pages will be pressed together on purpose, the theory being that this keeps the humidity from reaching the stamps; if this is tried, the album should still be opened often for examination and stamp airing.)

Strong direct light attacks stamps in a different way, by causing some colors to fade. It is not normally a problem, as there is no reason for stamps to be left in such a light. Now and then you will come across a dealer, however, who displays stamps in his window in sunlight; when buying from such a dealer be alert for possible color variances, which may be sunfading and not minor varieties.

A few general tips on storing stamps not in albums: Duplicates of any value should not be stored in bulk; protect their perforations by keeping them in stock books or glassines. Blocks should also be kept in glassines, a stiffening cardboard additionally being inserted with mint stamps to prevent them from curling. Use only philatelically acceptable materials with stored stamps—no wax paper, kitchen plastic wrap, or similar substances that can prove deleterious within a short time and are almost certain to be so over a long period. And if you have stamps in a safety deposit box, remember to check and air them regularly, too.

STRAIGHT EDGE

Straight Edge. In the printing of U.S. stamps from early times right up into the 1930s, no dividing gutters appeared between the four full panes on the press sheets. Consequently there was no space for perforation between the abutting rows of the separate individual panes, and when the sheet was cut each pane carried two adjacent rows of stamps each with one unperforated straight edge, one corner stamp on each pane having two straight edges, for a total of nineteen stamps so affected on every one-hundred-stamp pane. Straight edges spoil a stamp's appearance and lower its value, and their great disfavor among collectors was one of the reasons they were gradually eliminated in the U.S. by the addition of gutters on the sheets to separate the panes and allow full perforation. Straight edges have also appeared to a lesser extent on the stamps of other countries.

There are two opposite straight edges on the coil stamps of the United States and Canada, but they are not classed as straight edges in the above meaning; they appear on every coil stamp and are the identifying feature of the type. U.S. and Canadian stamps issued in booklet form also have one or more straight edges, such copies being less desirable than the regular fully perforated stamps; however, the U.S. 1970 eight-cent Eisenhower stamps (1395, 1402) and the 1975 thirteen-cent definitives (1595, 1618) are not available with full perforation, as they were issued only in coil and booklet forms, a practice that has also been followed with some later definitives.

Also see Booklet; Coil Stamps; Gutter; Pane.

Strip. Three or more stamps unseparated in a horizontal (usual) or vertical row.

Stuffed Cover. A mailed envelope containing only a stiffening piece of cardboard to give it body and help prevent damage to it in its travel through the postal system. Stiffeners are mainly inserted into first day and other special philatelic covers. They should be the proper size to fill the envelope exactly.

Superb. A grade of stamp condition. For descriptions of recognized grades, see Condition.

Surcharge. Usually, an additional amount added to a stamp by overprint to increase its face value. There are no U.S. surcharges. Four were issued in Canada in 1932, two being two-cent stamps surcharged to three cents (191, 191a) and two being five-cent airmails surcharged to six cents (C3–C4). Less common are surcharges that decrease a stamp's face value, as on two Canada 1899 issues (87–88) and two 1926 issues (139–140), all of which were three-cent stamps changed to two cents.

Also see Overprint.

Surtax. The amount earmarked for charity or other desig-nated cause that appears on semipostal stamps in addition

DECREASING SURCHARGE

to the postage denomination.

Also see Semipostal.

Susse Perforation. A coarse perforation (perf. 7) applied to some of the imperforate 1853–60 stamps of France (12–21) by a Paris commercial firm, the Susse Frères, as a convenience for their customers. The perforations were unofficial but are recognized in some catalogs, along with one or two official perforations of the same issue.

Sweat Box. Colloquial expression for humidifiers and humidors used to loosen hinges and other paper stuck to stamps.

Also see Humidifier.

Sydney Views. Popular name for the first stamps of New South Wales (1–9), issued in 1850 and 1851 and showing the colony's seal, part of which was believed to be a view of Sydney, the capital. Because of differences in paper, color, and most particularly the engravings themselves, this issue of three denominations rates nine separate catalog numbers with well over two hundred different collectible varieties and minor varieties. The series has long been a favorite study among students of British Commonwealth issues.

Syncopated Perforation. See Interrupted Perforation.

Tablet. An internal square or rectangle in a stamp's design carrying an inscription or denomination figure. Among the tablets that have appeared on U.S. stamps are the vertical ones on the inventors series (889–893) of the 1940 Famous Americans issue, showing subject name, stamp face value, and a symbolic device; and the horizontal one on the 1943 Four Freedoms issue (908), which carried the freedom quotation. One of the few examples of a true internal tablet on Canadian stamps is on the postage dues of 1933–34 (J11–J14), carrying the denomination. Tablets are common on foreign stamps, especially earlier ones.

Tagging. The application of luminescence to stamps to allow the use of electronic mail-processing machines. Tagging was introduced in Great Britain in 1959 and gradually adopted by other countries, including Canada in 1962 and the United States in 1963.

Also see Luminescence.

Taylor, Samuel A. (1838–1913). The most notorious American producer of fake stamps, which are not forgeries of existing issues but completely fictional stamps with no genuine counterparts. His active period was during the 1860s. Among his most brazen creations were a Paraguay stamp several years before the country even issued stamps, additional denominations for genuine issues of several countries, and in at least one instance a stamp bearing his own picture (a bogus U.S. local issue). Taylor was also the publisher of the first philatelic periodical in the United States, an apparently legitimate venture.

Telegraph Stamps. Stamps formerly used in many foreign countries for payment of telegraph charges. Mostly they were issued by private companies and have no philatelic standing, but in a few cases they were government stamps which in even fewer cases were also used sometimes to carry mail. In Spain postage stamps have served as telegraph stamps; those so used are distinguishable by a punched-out hole.

Tercentenary. A three-hundredth anniversary, often noted with a commemorative stamp issue. In the United States the tercentenary of the pilgrims' landing was marked in 1920 with three values (548–550) known for being the only U.S. stamps with the name of the country omitted; there have also been several tercentenary single stamps, including a few commemorating the founding of states. In 1966 Canada marked the three-hundredth anniversary of the arrival of the French explorer La Salle with a single stamp (446), but the country's best-known tercentenary issue is the popular Quebec Tercentenary eight-value series of 1908 (96–103).

CANADA QUEBEC TERCENTENARY

Tete-Beche. This French expression literally means head to spade, but is used idiomatically to mean top against bottom or head to tail. Philatelically the phrase refers to a stamp erroneously printed upside down in a pane, and the stamp must of course be collected still attached to at least one adjacent stamp to prove its tete-beche status. Tete-beches have appeared from time to time in several foreign countries, and many of the most expensive stamp rarities are tete-beche pairs or blocks.

Also see Rarities: France Tete-Beches, Bavaria Tete-Beche, Uruguay Tete-Beches.

Tied. Describes a canceled stamp on cover with the cancellation extending across both. In cases where counterfeit cancellations are known, a tied-to-cover stamp is more readily accepted as truly postally used than a loose stamp on which the cancellation could more easily have been forged. This pertains mostly to early stamps, and is a reason why early stamps tied to cover should usually be left that way.

Also see Cover.

Tin Hats. Popular name for a well-known stamp set of Belgium issued in 1919 to mark the end of World War I (126–137) and showing Belgian King Albert wearing a steel trench helmet.

Tongs. Stamp tongs are specially made for philatelic use with smooth gripping surfaces that do not harm paper, and for this reason are the only kinds of tongs that should be used with stamps. They are inexpensive (from under a dollar to a few dollars) and come in several types of ends including round, spade, pointed, and offset, the choice being a matter of personal taste; ends should be of thin-gauge metal to allow the tongs to slide easily under the stamps. Tongs should always be used in handling stamps (except when the stamps are wet from soaking—see Removing Paper from Stamps); they're easier to work with than fingers, and easier on the stamps too.

To Pay. An inscription appearing on the higher values of Great Britain postage dues to cover their secondary purpose, which is on packages mailed from abroad to denote the amount of customs duty payable.

Topical Collecting. Topical collecting is collecting by stamp subject or theme, as opposed, for instance, to country or era. A topical subject embraces persons, places, or things (explorers, animals, mountains, bridges, events, for example); a topical theme is more abstract and generally broader in scope (like education, space exploration, national security, entertainment). Often a stamp can fit in more than one topic; thus the U.S. 1975 Christmas stamp (1579) depicting Domenico Ghirlandaio's fifteenth-century painting *Madonna and Child* is pertinent in such subject categories as Christmas, paintings, and Italian artists, and in such theme categories as religion and motherhood.

The number of topics with enough stamps to make them challenging to collect is almost endless. In addition there are collectible subtopics within major topics. Instead of generalizing in all types of animals, for instance, it's entirely practical to collect only beasts of prey, or horses, or North American species. (For a listing of many topics and sub-topics, see section 5, "Topics for Topical Collecting.")

Topicalists enjoy the freedoms of selecting topics that most appeal to them and setting their own rules for the collection. It is natural, for example, for teachers to specialize in education, hunters in waterfowl, history buffs in statesmen. And since topicals are not a defined body of stamps, the topicalist can pursue his hobby however he sees fit. A caution to note, however, is that in recent years countless stamps have been issued almost entirely with the topical collector in mind, and with little or no postal justification for them; the practice is particularly common among the countries notorious for exploiting collectors. Most of these stamps are colorful and some are beautiful, and there is nothing wrong with a collector including them in his collection if he wishes; but he should be aware that they basically rank with seals and souvenirs and are almost certain to remain philatelically valueless.

The newcomer to topical collecting can choose from start-up packets in great variety, packets containing as many as one thousand different stamps being available in some categories (ships, paintings, birds, sports, to name a few). Expanding a collection needn't be expensive, because the topicalist seeks a subject or theme, not necessarily a specific stamp; at club exchanges, bourses, and dealers' stores he can browse through the penny stocks for anything pertinent he might find, an inexpensive form of philatelic pleasure otherwise enjoyed only by beginning collectors.

Because of the undefined nature of topical collecting, the topicalist has the further freedom of making album-page layouts and writing descriptive captions to suit his own tastes and purposes. For suggestions on these procedures, see Laying Out Attractive Album Pages, also Writeups and How to Prepare Them.

Traffic Lights. Popular name used mainly in Great Britain for the color dots appearing on the gutters of British stamp panes. The several colors used in producing the stamp are printed in a straight row of large dots resembling traffic lights. As printers' checks they are the counterparts of the color-plate numbers on the gutters of U.S. stamp panes.

Triangle Stamps. The first triangles, the original Cape of Good Hope issues of 1853–64 (1–15) attained early and long-lasting fame because of their unusual shape. All are scarce, and a few of the minor varieties—particularly the 1861 color errors, the one-penny blue (7b) and four-penny red (9b)—are rarities. A few other triangles were issued elsewhere during the same period, including the Newfoundland 1857 three-penny green (3) which is scarce but not rare. In recent years triangle stamps have come to be issued much more frequently, and they are often used to form specialized collections.

Trident. The first stamps of the Ukraine, issued in 1918 (1–61), were various Russian issues overprinted with an intricate trident design, the symbol of the temporarily independent region. The trident was also a prominent feature on most of the Ukraine's own stamps (62–74), which soon replaced the overprints. In 1923 the region became a Soviet republic and Russian stamps replaced the trident-bearing Ukrainian ones.

Trilingual. As used in philately, describes a stamp bearing three languages. The Canada 1977 Christmas issue (741–743) is an example of trilingualism, with the Huron Indian inscription JESOUS AHATONHIA as well as the English CHRIST-MAS and French NOËL appearing on all three stamps.

Triptych. A painting or other flat work of art on three panels side by side. Philatelically the term is used to describe such issues as the U.S. 1976 Spirit of '76 issue (1629–1631), consisting of a single picture perforated to form three separate stamps. In a similar treatment, the picture on the U.S. 1976 Declaration of Independence issue (1691–1694) yielded four individual stamps, a form known as a quadripartition.

Trucial States. A group of sheikdoms located along the south coast of the Persian Gulf, under British protection for many years until they formed the independent United Arab Emirates in 1971. Eleven Trucial States stamps were issued in 1961 and withdrawn in 1963 when the individual sheikdoms began issuing their own; these in turn were withdrawn in favor of United Arab Emirates stamps in 1972. The stamps issued before independence are usually grouped with the British Commonwealth, but many collectors do not consider them true Commonwealth issues; it is common for dealers to state in ads for Commonwealth packets or other offerings that no Trucials are included.

Type. As used in catalogs the term indicates a particular minor variety of a stamp issue, usually a slight variance in design. Such varieties are distinguished as Type I, Type II, etc. There are many instances of type varieties among U.S. issues through 1929, one stamp in particular—the two-cent Washington design of 1912–20—appearing in nine different versions. Type varieties are also listed occasionally for Canadian stamps.

Typeset. A stamp design made up of stock printing type and sometimes rules, and containing no artwork. Some early stamps were completely typeset, as are practically all overprints and surcharges.

Typography. See Printing Methods and How to Distinguish Them.

u. Abbreviation for used, commonly appearing in sale and auction catalogs in describing a stamp's condition. Used condition is also often indicated by the symbol⊙.

Umbrella Issues. Issues that contain enough different face values to make them practical for paying almost any postal charges with a minimum number of stamps. True umbrella issues usually consist of long definitive sets, but the U.S. 1893 Columbian issue with sixteen values from one cent to five dollars (230–245) and the Canada 1897 Diamond Jubilee issue with sixteen values from half-cent to five dollars (50–65) are examples of commemoratives that were also umbrella issues.

un. Abbreviation for unused, commonly appearing in sale and auction catalogs in describing a stamp's condition. Unused condition is also often indicated by an asterisk (*) or a star.

United States Postal Service. The branch of the U.S. government responsible for the mails, commonly abbreviated *USPS*. It was reorganized in 1971 to its present form as an independent agency headed by an appointed board of eleven governors, two of whom are the postmaster general and the deputy postmaster general. The USPS offers materials and services for collectors at many post offices and through its mail-order division in Washington, which also supplies new issues automatically by subscription. Address: United States Postal Service, Philatelic Sales Division, Washington, D.C. 20265.

Universal Postal Union. The international organization that makes it possible for mail to flow between countries as if there were no national borders separating them. Member nations accept incoming mail from other countries (subject to customs regulations on merchandise) and with no additional payment of postage merge it into their own mailstreams for delivery. The organization, which is commonly abbreviated *UPU*, was founded by twenty-one cooperating countries at Bern, Switzerland, in 1874, after receiving its initial impetus eleven years earlier in a Paris meeting arranged by President Lincoln's first postmaster general, Montgomery Blair. The United States was a charter member of the UPU in 1874, Canada joining in 1878; today there are something over 150 member nations, including all of any postal significance. In addition to expediting mail handling, the UPU has worked toward the establishment of simplification or uniformity in such areas as rates, weights, and stamp colors. It meets in congress every several years at irregularly spaced intervals, an event that has become an occasion for commemorative stamp emissions from many countries.

UPU. Universal Postal Union (see).

USPS. United States Postal Service (see).

Value. Value means either a stamp's face value (denomination) or catalog value (price). The term is used in both senses in this book, the intended meaning being apparent from the context.

Variety. Every individual stamp is a variety, either major or minor. A set of ten stamps, for instance, as in the U.S. 1934 National Parks issue (740–749), contains ten major varieties. Minor varieties are the result of slight variations in major varieties, common examples being in color shading; when they are recognized by catalogs—many are not—they bear their major variety's number followed by a distinguishing letter.

Very Fine, Very Good. Grades of stamp condition, commonly appearing in their abbreviated forms, *vf* and *vg*. For definitions of recognized grades, see Condition.

vf, vg. Very fine, very good (see).

Victorian. Categorizes the stamps issued during the reign of Queen Victoria by Great Britain and the Commonwealth countries, but used mostly to mean stamps of Great Britain itself.

Vignette. The central portion of a stamp's design containing a portrait or other illustration and enclosed within a line frame. The traditional vignette-in-frame concept was widely used during the nineteenth and through much of the twentieth century, but modern stamp design seldom follows this structured approach. Vignettes and frames as such have all but disappeared in favor of a billboard style of allover illustration, as can readily be seen on most U.S. and Canadian stamps issued since World War II.

Wallpaper. Colloquial expression for worthless stamps, especially those issued entirely or primarily to raise money from unknowing collectors. Some such emissions, even if they are from regular stamp-issuing countries, do not gain catalog listings. Most do, however, though there is little or no postal need for them; used-looking copies of such stamps are likely to have been canceled to order. There are also small entities throughout the world, including a few islands around Great Britain not permanently inhabited, that put out stamps claimed to be for payment of postage to the nearest legitimate post office, which of course doesn't make them postage stamps at all. The simple test for any questionable emission is whether by itself alone it is accepted to carry international mail; if not it is nothing more than a colored sticker. Topical collectors in particular should beware of current wallpaper, much of which is produced with them in mind; topical-oriented stamps are mostly colorful and attractive, and deal with any salable subject that may or may not have direct relationship to the issuing country.

There have been countless past examples of wallpaper, in most cases theoretically admissible stamps including (but by no means limited to) some early issues of Liberia and Persia; the runaway-inflation surcharges of Germany following World War I; German, Italian, and Russian stamps of the 1930s and World War II; and the notorious Seebeck issues of Central and South America. And there are occasional modern issues from philatelically respected countries that in the opinion of many collectors and stamp societies are practically wallpaper although they attain catalog status and have some value; they consist largely of unjustifiable commemoratives, superfluous definitives, or unneeded high denominations.

Also see Canceled to Order; Seebeck Issues; Surcharge.

Want List. As its name implies, a want list is a collector's enumeration of stamps required to fill his album spaces. While it need be nothing more than a listing in a notebook, some collectors prefer to keep it in the form of an inventory record in one of the various inexpensive pocket-size books available for the purpose; such books typically allow space for recording individual stamps new and used, blocks, and acquisition costs. A want list is of course a necessity for a collector randomly shopping a dealer's stock book or a club swap book, and many collectors find it efficient to put their lists into the hands of mail-order dealers from whom they receive approvals.

War-Tax Stamps. Stamps issued during World War I by most British Commonwealth countries to help raise money for the war effort, usually by means of a surcharge on regular postage stamps. In Canada, one-cent and two-cent George V definitives were used for the purpose, in 1915 by the addition of the words WAR TAX and in 1916 and later by a one-cent surcharge. Neither of these notations was an overprint, both being struck into the stamps' regular design before printing. There were four major Canadian war-tax varieties, plus others with differences in dies and perforations, for a total of ten recognized numbers (MR1–MR7a). Most are common used; a few are expensive unused.

Watermark. A watermark, which appears as a translucent design in paper, is actually a thinning of the paper produced by a metal form during the papermaking process. Watermarks were originally used because they were felt to be a deterrent against forgery. While they have many details of interest to the watermark specialist, the general collector needs to know only which watermark design, if any, appears in the stamp (in Great Britain, for example, many stamps otherwise identical have been issued with differing watermarks and are assigned separate catalog numbers); the watermark information is given in catalog listings.

Watermarks generally are of minor significance in today's stamps. Either they don't exist at all, or if they do they're meaningless for identification or value setting because stamps now are rarely issued in both watermarked and unwatermarked versions.

United States. In the United States watermarks were used between 1895 and 1917. They appeared in two versions of the letters USPS, one in double-line outline, the other in plain single lines. The letters are repeated in large size across the sheet, not together in their entirety in each stamp; any individual stamp thus contains only a portion of a letter. The only U.S. watermark since 1917 occurred in error on some copies of the one dollar value in the Presidential issue of 1938 (832b), the error being somewhat common used and somewhat scarce unused.

Canada. The only watermarked stamps ever issued by Canada were eight values of the Queen Victoria definitives of 1868–79 (21b–30d, not inclusive). This series also appeared unwatermarked and in several other variations. There are two different watermarks and they are not official designs but commercial, being the names of the paper manufacturers. All of the eight watermarked stamps are rare, especially unused; 21b is one of Canada's most expensive numbers.

Watermark Detecting. A watermark can sometimes be discerned simply by looking for it on the back of the stamp, and sometimes by holding the stamp to a light. Usually, however, watermarks are revealed only with the aid of a watermark detector and liquid. The detector is an inexpensive shallow black tray on which the stamp is laid face down and touched with a few drops of the liquid, which immediately saturates it and almost as quickly disappears by evaporation. In the few intervening seconds the watermark normally becomes momentarily visible against the black of the tray. Watermark liquids should be used with caution, since they are usually benzine-based products—volatile, highly flammable, and dangerous to inhale; in addition, they can cause stamps printed by photogravure or with fugitive inks to run. (In recent years watermark liquids not of the benzine type have been made available, and are said to be less likely to harm vulnerable stamps.) There are also detection methods utilizing color filters and light; they can be somewhat expensive and complex for the average collector, and there is no unanimous agreement on their degree of effectiveness.

Not all watermarks appear readily in the detecting process. If a mark doesn't show with the first application of liquid, try another and be prepared to look sharp; some marks appear most clearly in the instant they are first touched by the liquid. Be sure to work under a good light, and it helps to know exactly what you're looking for, although this isn't always possible; for example, some of the pre-1867 issues of Great Britain might have any one of three different watermarks on stamps otherwise identical. But even with the most careful study, some watermarks remain elusive. Well-known frustrating examples are the single-line *USPS* marks of the United States, which in some positions on the stamps can be almost impossible to detect. If detection becomes important enough to warrant payment of a fee, the best solution is to buy expert opinion (see Expertising).

Wells, Fargo & Co. A transportation company that carried passengers and express by stagecoach in the American West starting in 1852. In 1861 the company issued private stamps for mail forwarded by the Pony Express, for which it was an agent; the genuine stamps are rare (forgeries abound) and unlisted by most general catalogs, but in demand among postal-history specialists. A fact not widely known is that although the name Wells Fargo has come to be almost synonymous with Old West, the company was established and had its headquarters in the unlikely eastern city of Buffalo, New York, where its original site is now marked by a plaque on a downtown building.

Also see Pony Express.

Wing Margin. On pre-1880 perforated stamps of Great Britain, the central gutters in full stamp panes were perforated only through the middle of the gutter instead of at each edge close to the stamps, as is done now. This left a wide unprinted margin, known as a wing margin, on all stamps abutting gutters. It also gave stamps with wing margins a shape unsuited to standard album spaces, making them unpopular with collectors. To overcome this the stamps were often trimmed to standard size and reperforated by philatelic trade suppliers, but the modified stamps are easily detected by their corner letters, which appeared on all Great Britain issues until 1887 and made it possible to calculate every stamp's position in the pane.

Also see Corner Letters.

Wove Paper. See Paper Types and How to Distinguish Them.

Writeups and How to Prepare Them. A writeup is a descriptive note written by the collector and entered with a stamp or group of stamps on an album page. It can also take the form of an introduction to a collection or a section thereof. There is no need for writeups in collections by country mounted in printed albums, for the albums themselves carry identification of issues, which is all that is normally desirable for basic collections. Specialized and topical collections, however, are improved by writeups, but the writeups should be used judiciously. Their purpose is simply to provide helpful information or explanation to the collection's viewers; they should be used only when necessary to achieve this purpose and must remain secondary to the stamps. Writeups are also needed, if only to set forth objectives, on pages exhibited at shows or entered in competition. In all cases they should be composed before the pages are laid out so proper space can be left for them.

Writing Tips. Be factual, and as brief as possible. Don't waste words on obvious things like a stamp's denomination and color, and don't try to cover everything about a stamp— mention only details that are pertinent to the collection's purpose. In a topical collection of paintings, for example, these could be no more than the artist's name, dates, and nationality; the title and date of the work; and its present location. If a collection is concerned with one particular aspect of philatelic study, choose the writeup data accordingly; typical kinds of data include the reason for a stamp's issue, design subject matter, printing method, and details regarding paper, watermark, perforation, and other production factors. From this it can be seen that the same stamp would be treated differently in different collections. As an example, the U.S. 1909 Hudson-Fulton Celebration stamp issued both perforate and imperforate (372–373) might be variously written up as follows for the types of collections noted:

■ Commemorative: "Issued 1909 to mark the three-hundredth anniversary of the Hudson River's discovery and the one-hundred-second anniversary of the first river trip of Robert Fulton's steamship *Clermont*."

- Topical, Ships: "Hudson River navigation at the Palisades in 1807 by Indian canoe, the sailing vessel *Half Moon*, and the first steamship, Robert Fulton's *Clermont.*"

- Watermark: "The United States has used only two watermarks, the single-line USPS and the double-line USPS. This 1909 commemorative stamp carries a portion of the letter *P* in the double-line version."

- Perforation (with both varieties mounted): "The third of three U.S. stamps issued in 1909 both perforated and imperforate; the other two were the Lincoln Memorial and Alaska-Yukon Pacific Exposition issues." (Don't make a redundant statement like "An example of a single stamp issued both perforate and imperforate," which would be wasting words on the obvious.)

Note that twenty-five to thirty words should in most cases be ample for a single stamp or a single-purpose set. Writeups that serve as collection introductions or descriptions can be somewhat longer, but should seldom require more than one hundred words. Their objective is to explain what the collection demonstrates and what materials will be displayed as documentation; or to give biographical or background information about its subject whether a person, place, thing, or event; or to set the stage for a theme to be presented and discussed philatelically; or to make some other general statement about the collection. The guidelines for writing these longer entries are the same as for the shorter ones: Stick to what's factual and pertinent, and use words economically, for they pile up fast—this paragraph alone contains about 135 of them.

Getting Facts. It goes without saying that all information given in a writeup must be accurate, and hence it's important to know where to seek facts and where to check them. The basic things having to do with a stamp's production—paper, watermark, printing method, etc.—are not a problem, as they are given in catalogs, often with additional details concerning them. For skeletal historical facts or descriptions of subjects depicted on stamps, check any good dictionary, where you will find most subjects covered with a line or two; the annual almanacs also give such data, especially on persons and places. Then come general encyclopedias, specialized encyclopedias, and published literature on the person or topic; these sources are available at your public library.

Stamp subjects that do not have encyclopedia entries of their own may appear in a kindred entry (the British painter George Stubbs, whose painting *Mares and Foals* illustrated the Great Britain nine-penny stamp in the 1967 British Paintings issue (515), is for instance mentioned in the *Encyclopedia Americana* only under *Great Britain: Fine Arts*); so you should always check the subject in an encyclopedia's index for possible reference to a different heading. If a subject doesn't appear in a general encyclopedia at all, go to a specialized one dealing with the appropriate theme, provided there is such a one, or to relevant library shelf books. Examples of commemorated people for whom you may have to dig as deep as this are nurse Clara Maass (U.S. 1699) and credit unionist Alphonse Desjardins (Canada 661); but it's safe to say that anybody or anything ever honored on a stamp is important enough to be found somewhere among the books on a library's shelves. In any case you are never looking for a host of facts on a subject, but only for the few significant ones, as shown in the following examples of a typical simple writeup for a person, a place, a thing, and an event:

■ Louisa May Alcott, U.S. 862: "Louisa May Alcott 1832–88, the American writer best known for her girls' classic *Little Women*, wrote numerous sketches and adult novels in addition to her juvenile works."

■ Great Bear Lake, Canada 269: "Great Bear Lake, located in Canada's Northwest Territories and covering 12,000 square miles, is the world's eighth largest lake, larger than Erie and Ontario of the Great Lakes."

■ Stephen Daye printing press, U.S. 857: "The English immigrant Stephen Daye (1594–1668) brought this printing press with him in 1638 to Cambridge, Massachusetts, where it operated as the first press in the American colonies."

■ 1871 Census Centennial, Canada 542: "The 1871 census, the first national one following Canadian Confederation, showed a population of 3.7 million not including Manitoba, Saskatchewan, Newfoundland, or the Yukon, which had not yet been admitted."

These writeups are the type that would be suitable for merely providing basic information about a stamp's subject. For collections with a specific title—say Famous Novels,

Water as a Resource, A History of Early Printing, or Centennials on Stamps—they would be slanted to the title, as exemplified in the previous Hudson-Fulton samples. If the research may sometimes seem like a lot of work to glean such a few usable facts, keep in mind that writeups would be valueless without those few facts. And you'll find the search for them to be its own reward—it's one of the most interesting aspects of stamp collecting.

Entering Tips. Use taste and care in entering writeups on the page. They should not appear in garish colors or be unduly ornamented, although a simple line box around a writeup is effective especially if in a color complementing the stamps on the page. Typewritten copy is best; hand lettering—which should be all capitals—is acceptable if carefully done; handwriting, unless it's exceptionally fine, is least desirable. Experiment with the fit of the copy and the line breaks on a separate paper before you enter the writeup on the page. Text is almost always best in black; for typewritten work, do not use a grayed-out ribbon. To avoid damaging stamps, enter the writeups in their allotted places before you mount the stamps on the page.

Finally, remember that writeups are one of the ways by which you give the collection a personal flavor, and many of the above are guidelines, not hard rules. Set as your goals writing informative copy and tastefully entering it, and your pages will both please you and interest your collection's viewers.

Also see Competition Exhibiting; Laying Out Attractive Album Pages.

YACHT KEY TYPE

Yachts. Popular name for 1900–1919 stamps of several German colonies and protectorates, issued in two designs and so called because both designs showed the kaiser's yacht *Hohenzollern.* The stamps were key types issued by Germany and differing only in the inscribed name of the colony. Some were overprinted by British or French occupation forces during World War I.

Also see Key Type.

Year Set. The stamps issued by a single country in a single year, usually but not always excluding definitives, and frequently offered as a complete set by dealers. Year sets generally comprise only regular stamps, and not airmails, postage dues, or other special-purpose issues.

Zeppelins. Generally, the popular name for stamps issued by many countries to mark the use of German zeppelins and other dirigibles in carrying mail. In particular, the term refers to the well-known U.S. 1930 Graf Zeppelin airmail issue of three stamps (C13–C15). This set remained in little demand for several years, one reason being its high denominations for depression times (65 cents, $1.30, $2.60). Eventually, though, it gained in acceptance and now ranks consistently among the most popular U.S. issues. None of the three stamps is rare, but all are expensive both unused and used.

Z-Grill. One of several types of grills used on U.S. postage stamps between 1867 and 1871 in an experiment to prevent cancellation removal and stamp reuse. The Z-grill is the best known of the types because three of the six stamps it was used on are among the rarest U.S. issues (85a, 85d, 85f).

Also see Grill; Rarities; U.S. Franklin Z-Grill.

Zurich Numerals. Popular name for stamps issued in 1843 in the Swiss canton of Zurich, so called because their denomination numeral was the overwhelming feature of the design. They were issued in two major varieties of two denominations each (1L1–1L4), and also in minor varieties and reprints. All are scarce, and the two four-rappen denominations (1L1 and 1L3) are rarities.

U.S. ZEPPELIN AIRMAIL

ZURICH NUMERAL

Practically every stamp-issuing country maintains an official outlet for the sale of its stamps and other philatelic items to collectors. The services available from these agencies (automatic new-issue shipments, first day covers, canceling to order, to name a few examples) vary from country to country and in some cases from time to time, as do terms of payment and other conditions of sale; for these reasons no attempt is made here to do more than provide a complete mailing address for each agency. From this, if ever you contemplate dealing with any of them, you can obtain timely and correct information by direct inquiry.

Since other countries are likely to have business practices different from ours—and a majority of the agencies a language different from ours—these few correspondence guidelines should be generally followed:

1. In contacting foreign-speaking countries use clear, simple language and sentence construction, avoiding idiomatic expressions that could be misconstrued. Interpreters are not necessarily expert; many of them do little more than substitute word for word, a practice that because of idiom can result in misunderstandings. (Examples of interpretation pitfalls are often seen in ambiguous and sometimes unintentionally humorous phrases in instructions accompanying Japanese-made goods, the words being English but the idiom Japanese.)

2. Foreign handwriting styles can be different from ours (for instance Europeans write the figure 1 with a top hook that makes it look like our 7, and distinguish the 7 by drawing

a horizontal line through the stem); thus it is better to print than to write, and of course best of all to type.

3. If you give your name and address by means of a printed sticker without country name, be sure to complete your address by adding the country.

4. When inquiring, always ask the required method of remittance, and whether your currency or that of the foreign country is preferred. Most countries accept U.S. dollars and almost as many accept Canadian dollars, but a few prefer their own money. Postal and international money orders are common means of transmittal—avoid mailing cash.

5. Unless you're willing to wait several months for response, use airmail and ask the agency to reply the same way; surface mail can take weeks in each direction. (Actually you may have a long wait in any case; some agencies can be as slow as some domestic mail-order houses.)

6. With your original inquiry enclose one or more international reply coupons, available at post offices, to encourage a prompt reply from the agency. Your post office should be able to tell you if more than one coupon is needed to prepay an airmail reply from the particular country involved. Reply coupons should not be necessary after the first time, as prices normally include postage.

All of this is not meant to imply that dealing with foreign philatelic agencies is a complicated affair, which it really isn't; the agencies are, after all, in business to develop and serve customers. But as with any business dealings, misunderstandings can be minimized and satisfaction maximized by adhering to sound practices.

The list that follows does not include every philatelic agency throughout the world, but the omissions are comparatively few and are intentional in each case for one of these three reasons: An agency might deal only in wholesale quantities to the trade and not at retail to individual collectors, its country's goods including stamps may have been embargoed by the United States, or it may represent a tiny entity whose postally unneeded stamps have little or no interest for the average collector. But from the user's practical standpoint, the listing can be considered virtually complete.

ABU DHABI   Philatelic Bureau, GPO
                    Dubai, United Arab Emirates ·

ADEN	Director General of P&T, Postal Division Aden, Yemen People's Democratic Republic
AFGHANISTAN	Director of Posts, Philatelic Section Kabul, Afghanistan
AITUTAKI	Aitutaki Post Office Aitutaki, Cook Islands South Pacific
AJMAN	Philatelic Bureau, GPO Dubai, United Arab Emirates
ALBANIA	Exportal Rue 4 Shkurt Tirana, Albania
ALGERIA	Receveur Principal des PTT, Service Philatelique Algiers R.P., Algeria
ANDORRA (French)	Service Philatelique des PT 61 Rue de Douai 75436 Paris, France
ANDORRA (Spanish)	Servicio Filatelico, Direccion General de Correos Madrid 14, Spain
ANGOLA	Centro Filatelico Largo da Republica, C.P. 2688 Luanda, Angola
ANGUILLA	Department of Posts The Valley Anguilla, West Indies (also see Saint Kitts-Nevis-Anguilla)
ANTIGUA	Philatelic Bureau, GPO St. John's, Antigua West Indies
ARGENTINA	Seccion Filatelica, Correos Central Avenida Corrientes Buenos Aires, Argentina
ASCENSION	Postmaster General Jamestown, Saint Helena Island South Atlantic
AUSTRALIA	Philatelic Bureau P.O. Box 9000 Melbourne, Victoria 3001 Australia

AUSTRIA	Österreichische Post Briefmarkenversandstelle A-1011 Vienna, Austria
BAHAMAS	Postmaster GPO Box N8302 Nassau, Bahamas
BAHRAIN	Philatelic Bureau, Director of Posts Bahrain, Arabian Gulf
BANGLADESH	Senior Postmaster, Dacca GPO Dacca, Bangladesh
BARBADOS	Philatelic Bureau, GPO Bridgetown, Barbados West Indies
BARBUDA	Philatelic Bureau, GPO Codrington, Barbuda West Indies
BASUTOLAND	see Lesotho
BECHUANALAND	see Botswana
BELGIAN CONGO	see Congo Republic
BELGIUM	Regie des Postes, Bureau des Collectionneurs Rue de Cirque 25 1000 Brussels, Belgium
BELIZE (formerly British Honduras)	Philatelic Bureau, GPO Belmopan, Belize
BENIN	Agence Philatelique, Office des PTT Porto-Novo, Dahomey Benin Republic
BERMUDA	Philatelic Bureau, GPO Hamilton, Bermuda
BHUTAN	Philatelic Bureau, GPO Thimbu, Bhutan
BOLIVIA	Direccion Nacional de Correos, Seccion Filatelica La Paz, Bolivia
BOTSWANA	Department of Posts and Telegraphs Gaberones, Botswana
BRAZIL	Empresa de Correios y Telegrafos, Central Filatelica Caixa Postal 04-400 70 000 Brasilia, DF Brazil

194

BRITISH ANTARCTICA	Postmaster for British Antarctic Territory, GPO Port Stanley, Falkland Islands
BRITISH GUIANA	see Guyana
BRITISH HONDURAS	see Belize
BRITISH INDIAN OCEAN TERRITORY	Postmaster General, GPO Victoria, Seychelles
BRITISH VIRGIN ISLANDS	Postmaster General, Philatelic Bureau Road Town, Tortola British Virgin Islands
BRUNEI	Postal Services Department, GPO Bandar Seri Begawan, Brunei
BULGARIA	Service Philatelique Postal 44 Dencoglou Sofia, Bulgaria
BURMA	Posts and Telecommunications, Philatelic Section Rangoon, Burma
BURUNDI	Agence Philatelique Boite Postale 45 Bujumbura, Burundi
CAMEROON	Receveur General des PTT Yaounde, Cameroon
CANADA	Philatelic Service, Canada Post Ottawa, Ontario K1A 0B5
CANAL ZONE	Canal Zone Postal Service, Philatelic Agency Balboa, Canal Zone
CAPE VERDE ISLANDS	Servicos dos Correios, GPO Praia, Cape Verde Islands
CAYMAN ISLANDS	Postmaster, Philatelic Department Grand Cayman, Cayman Islands
CENTRAL AFRICAN EMPIRE	Service Philatelique des PTT Bangui, Central African Republic
CEYLON	see Sri Lanka
CHAD	Receveur General des PTT Ndjamena, Chad
CHILE	Direccion Nacional de Correos y Telecomunicacion Subdireccion de Correos, Departamento Filatelico Santiago 21, Chile

CHINA REPUBLIC (TAIWAN)	Philatelic Department, Directorate General of Posts Taipei 106, Taiwan Republic of China
CHRISTMAS ISLAND	Philatelic Bureau Christmas Island
COLOMBIA	Oficina Filatelica, Administracion Postal Nacional 209 Edificio Murillo Toro Bogota, DE Colombia
COMORO ISLANDS	Direction Generale des PTT, Service Philatelique Moroni, Comoro Islands
CONGO REPUBLIC (formerly Belgian Congo)	Agences Philateliques Gouvernementales 868 Chaussee de Waterloo 1180 Brussels, Belgium
CONGO PEOPLE'S REPUBLIC (formerly French Congo)	Direction Generale des PTT, Service Philatelique Brazzaville, Congo People's Republic
COOK ISLANDS	Philatelic Bureau Box 200 Raratonga, Cook Islands
COSTA RICA	Direccion General de Correos, Oficina Filatelica San Jose, Costa Rica
CURACAO	see Netherlands Antilles
CYPRUS	Philatelic Branch, GPO Nicosia, Cyprus
DAHOMEY	Agence Philatelique, Office des PTT Porto-Novo, Dahomey Benin Republic
DENMARK	Postens Filateli 59 Raadhuspladsen DK-1550 Copenhagen V, Denmark
DJIBOUTI (formerly Afars & Issas)	Service Philatelique, Direction Generals des PTT Djibouti, Republic of Djibouti
DOMINICA	Stamp Order Division, GPO Roseau, Dominica West Indies
DOMINICAN REPUBLIC	Oficina Filatelica, Direccion General de Correos Santo Domingo, Dominican Republic

DUBAI	Philatelic Bureau, GPO Dubai, United Arab Emirates
ECUADOR	Departamento Filatelico, Museo Postal del Estado Direccion General de Correos, Correo Central Quito, Ecuador
EGYPT	Philatelic Office, Postal Department Cairo, Arab Republic of Egypt
ETHIOPIA	Post Office Department, Philatelic Section P.O. Box 1112 Addis Ababa, Ethiopia
FALKLAND ISLANDS	Philatelic Bureau, GPO Port Stanley, Falkland Islands
FAEROE ISLANDS	Postal Service, Philatelic Office 38001 Torshavn, Faroe Islands
FIJI	Philatelic Bureau 64 Victoria Parade Suva, Fiji
FINLAND	Philatelic Section, General Direction of Posts and Telecommunications Box 654 00101 Helsinki 10, Finland
FRANCE	Service Philatelique des Postes et Telecommunications 61 Rue de Douai 75436 Paris, France
FRENCH COLONIES	Agence des Timbres Poste d'Outre-Mer 85 Avenue de la Bourdonnais 75007 Paris, France
FRENCH POLYNESIA	Receveur Principale des PTT, Poste Centrale Papeete, Tahiti French Polynesia
FUJEIRA	Philatelic Bureau, GPO Dubai, United Arab Emirates
GABON	Service Philatelique, Direction General des PTT Libreville, Gabon
GAMBIA	Postmaster General, GPO Bathurst, The Gambia
GHANA	Philatelic Bureau, Department of Posts Accra, Ghana

GIBRALTAR	Philatelic Bureau, GPO
	Box 5662
	Gibraltar
GILBERT AND ELLICE ISLANDS	Philatelic Bureau
	Box 494
	Betio, Tarawa
	Gilbert and Ellice Islands
GOLD COAST	see Ghana
GREAT BRITAIN	British Post Office Philatelic Bureau
	2 Waterloo Place
	Edinburgh EH1 1AB, Scotland
GREECE	Post Office Philatelic Service
	100 Aeoulou Street
	Athens 131, Greece
GREENLAND	Gronlands Postvaesen
	100 Strandgade
	DK-1004 Copenhagen K, Denmark
GRENADA	Postmaster General, GPO
	St. George's, Grenada
	West Indies
GUATEMALA	Departamento Filatelico, Correos Central
	Guatemala City, Guatemala
GUERNSEY	Philatelic Bureau, Head Post Office
	St. Peter Port, Guernsey
	Channel Islands
GUINEA	Agence Philatelique
	B.P. 814
	Conakry, Republic of Guinea
GUYANA	Philatelic Bureau, GPO
	Georgetown, Guyana
HAITI	Office du Timbre, Administration Generale des Contributions
	P.O. Box 3
	Port-au-Prince, Haiti
HONDURAS	Oficina Filatelica, Direccion General de Correos
	Correos Central
	Tegucigalpa, Honduras
HONG KONG	Philatelic Bureau, GPO
	Hong Kong Island, Hong Kong

ICELAND	Frimerkjasalan Post Box 1445 Reykjavik, Iceland
INDIA	Philatelic Bureau, GPO Bombay 400 001, Maharashtra India
INDONESIA	Philatelic Subdivision, State Posts and Giro 34 Jalan Jakarta Bandung, Java Indonesia
IRAN	Directorate General of Posts, Philatelic Bureau Tehran, Iran
IRAQ	Philatelic Bureau, Posts and Savings Administration Baghdad, Iraq
IRELAND	Philatelic Section, GPO Dublin 1, Ireland
ISLE OF MAN	Philatelic Bureau, Post Office Authority Box 10M Douglas, Isle of Man
ISRAEL	Ministry of Communications, Philatelic Services Tel Aviv-Yafo 61 080, Israel
ITALY	Ufficio Principale Filatelico Via Mario de Fiori 00100 Rome, Italy
IVORY COAST	Direction Generale des PTT, Service Philatelique Abidjan, Ivory Coast
JAMAICA	Philatelic Bureau, GPO Kingston, Jamaica
JAPAN	Central Post Office, Philatelic Section CPO Box 888 Tokyo 100-91, Honshu Japan
JERSEY	Post Office Philatelic Bureau Box 304 St. Helier, Jersey Channel Islands
JORDAN	Service Philatelique, Direction Generale des PTT Amman, Jordan

KENYA	East African P&T, Department of Posts Box 30301 Nairobi, Kenya
KUWAIT	Philatelic Section, GPO Kuwait City, Kuwait
LAOS	Service Philatelique des PTT Vientiane, Laos
LEBANON	Receveur Principal des Postes, Service Philatelique Beirut, Lebanon
LESOTHO	Philatelic Bureau Box 413 Maseru, Lesotho
LIBERIA	Liberian Philatelic Agency 261 Broadway New York, N.Y. 10007
LIBYA	Direction Generale des PTT, Service Philatelique Tripoli, Libya
LIECHTENSTEIN	Official Philatelic Service FL-9490 Vaduz, Liechtenstein
LUXEMBOURG	Direction des Postes, Office des Timbres Boite 999 Luxembourg, Luxembourg
MACAO	Postmaster, Philatelic Department Macao, Macao
MALAGASY REPUBLIC	Direction Generale des PTT, Service Philatelique Tananarive-RP, Madagascar Malagasy Republic
MALAWI	Philatelic Bureau, Department of P&T Box 1000 Blantyre, Malawi
MALAYSIA	Director General of Posts Kuala Lumpur, Malaya Malaysia
MALDIVE ISLANDS	Philatelic Bureau, GPO Male, Maldive Island
MALI	Service Philatelique, Direction Generale des PTT Bamako, Mali

MALTA	Philatelic Bureau, GPO
	Valletta, Malta
MAURITANIA	Service Philatelique, Direction Generals des PTT
	BP 99
	Nouakchott, Mauritania
MAURITIUS	Department of Posts and Telegraphs, GPO
	Port Louis, Mauritius
MEXICO	Oficina Filatelica, Edificio de Correos
	Mexico City 1, D.F.
	Mexico
MONACO	Office des Emissions des Timbres-Postes, Department des Finances
	Monaco
MONTSERRAT	Philatelic Bureau, GPO
	Plymouth, Montserrat
	West Indies
MOROCCO	Ministere des PTT, Division Postale
	Rabat, Morocco
MOZAMBIQUE	Seccao Filatelica, Servicos dos Correios
	Lourenço Marques, Mozambique
MUSCAT AND OMAN	see Oman
NEPAL	Philatelic Bureau, GPO
	Kathmandu, Nepal
NETHERLANDS	Post Office Philatelic Service
	Prinses Beatrixlaan 11
	The Hague, The Netherlands
NETHERLANDS ANTILLES	Postal Administration Philatelic Service
	Willemstad, Curacao
	Netherlands Antilles
NEW CALEDONIA	Service Philatelique, Direction Generale des PTT
	Noumea, New Caledonia
NEW HEBRIDES	Philatelic Section, Condominium Post Office
	Vila, New Hebrides Islands
NEW ZEALAND	Post Office Philatelic Bureau
	Private Bag
	Wanganui, New Zealand
NICARAGUA	Oficina de Control de Postales y Filatelia
	Apartado 325, Palacio Nacional
	Managua, Nicaragua

NIGER	Service Philatelique, Direction Generale des PTT Niamey, Republic of Niger
NIGERIA	Philatelic Service, GPO P.M.B. 12647 Lagos, Nigeria
NORWAY	Postens Filatelitjeneste Sentrum Oslo 1, Norway
OMAN	Philatelic Bureau, Department of PTT Muscat, Oman
PAKISTAN	Philatelic Bureau, GPO Karachi, Pakistan
PANAMA	Direccion General de Correos, Departamento de Filatelia Apartado 3421 Panama City 1, Panama
PAPUA NEW GUINEA	Philatelic Bureau Box 160 Port Moresby, Papua New Guinea
PARAGUAY	Oficina Filatelica, Direccion General de Correos Asuncion, Paraguay
PERU	Philatelic Postal Museum, GPO Lima, Peru
PHILIPPINES	Philatelic Division, Bureau of Posts Manila, Philippines
PORTUGAL	Philatelic Office, Portuguese P&T Rua Alves Redol Lisbon 1, Portugal
QATAR	Philatelic Bureau, Department of Posts Doha, Qatar
REUNION	Service Philatelique des Postes et Telecommunications 61 Rue de Douai 75436 Paris, France
ROMANIA	ILEXIM 3 Decembrie Street Bucharest, Romania
RWANDA	Agences Philateliques Gouvernementales 868 Chaussee de Waterloo 1180 Brussels, Belgium

SAINT KITTS-NEVIS- ANGUILLA	Philatelic Department, GPO Basseterre, Saint Kitts West Indies
SAINT LUCIA	Postmaster General, GPO Castries, Saint Lucia West Indies
SAINT PIERRE AND MIQUELON	Service Philatelique, Direction Generale des PTT Saint Pierre, Saint Pierre and Miquelon
SAINT VINCENT	Philatelic Services, GPO Kingstown, Saint Vincent West Indies
EL SALVADOR	Direccion General de Correos, Departamento de Filatelia 2 Avenida Espana San Salvador, El Salvador
SAN MARINO	Philatelic Office Republic of San Marino
SAUDI ARABIA	Division of Posts and Telegraphs, Philatelic Section Riyadh, Saudi Arabia
SENEGAL	Service Philatelique, Direction Generale des PTT Dakar, Republic of Senegal
SEYCHELLES	Postmaster General, GPO Box 60 Victoria, Seychelles
SHARJAH	Philatelic Bureau, GPO Dubai, United Arab Emirates
SIERRA LEONE	Postmaster General, GPO Freetown, Sierra Leone
SINGAPORE	Philatelic Bureau, GPO Singapore 1, Singapore
SOLOMON ISLANDS	Philatelic Bureau, GPO Honiara, Guadalcanal Solomon Islands
SOMALIA	Philatelic Section, Ministry of Posts and Telecommunications Mogadiscio, Somalia
SOUTH AFRICA	Philatelic Services, GPO Pretoria 0001, Republic of South Africa

SOUTH GEORGIA	Philatelic Bureau, GPO Port Stanley, Falkland Islands
SOUTH KOREA	Philatelic Center Box 495 Seoul 100, Republic of Korea
SOUTH WEST AFRICA (Namibia)	Philatelic Services, GPO Pretoria 0001, Republic of South Africa
SPAIN	Servicio Filatelico de Correos, Direccion General de Correos Madrid 14, Spain
SPANISH EQUATORIAL GUINEA	Philatelic Office, Filatelia Africana SL Jorge Juan 51 Madrid 1, Spain
SPANISH SAHARA	Servicio Filatelico de Correos, Direccion General de Correos Madrid 14, Spain
SRI LANKA	Philatelic Bureau Ceylinco House Colombo 1, Sri Lanka
SUDAN	Philatelic Section, Posts and Telegraphs Department Khartoum, Sudan
SURINAM	Postal Administration, Philatelic Department Paramaribo, Surinam
SWAZILAND	Stamp Bureau, Department of Posts and Telecommunications Mbabane, Swaziland
SWEDEN	Postens Frimarksavelning, PFA S-10502 Stockholm, Sweden
SWITZERLAND	Philatelic Bureau, PTT Parkterrasse 10 CH-3030 Bern, Switzerland
SYRIA	Etablissement des Postes et Telecommunications, Service Philatelique Damascus, Syria
TAIWAN	see China Republic
TANZANIA	Department of Posts, East African P&T Box 9070 Dar es Salaam, Tanzania
THAILAND	Philatelic Promotion Centre, Posts and Telegraphs Bangkok 5, Thailand

TIMOR	Postmaster's Office, Philatelic Section Dili, Portuguese Timor Timor
TOGO	Service Philatelique, Direction General des PTT Lomé, Togo
TRINIDAD AND TOBAGO	Philatelic Department, GPO Port of Spain, Trinidad
TUNISIA	Service Philatelique des PTT, Recette Principale Tunis, Tunisia
TURKEY	Direction Generale des PTT, Section des Timbres Postes Ankara, Turkey
TURKS AND CAICOS ISLANDS	Postmaster's Office, Philatelic Department Grand Turk, Turks and Caicos Islands
UGANDA	Department of Posts, East African P&T Box 7171 Kampala, Uganda
UMM AL-QUAIWAIN	Philatelic Bureau, GPO Dubai, United Arab Emirates
UNITED ARAB EMIRATES	Philatelic Bureau, GPO Dubai, United Arab Emirates
UNITED NATIONS	United Nations Postal Administration Box 5900, Grand Central Station New York, N.Y. 10017
UNITED STATES	United States Postal Service, Philatelic Sales Division Washington, D.C. 20265
UPPER VOLTA	Service Philatelique, Office des P&T Ouagadougou, Upper Volta
URUGUAY	Direccion Nacional de Correos, Oficina Filatelica 1296 Casilla de Correos Montevideo, Uruguay
VATICAN CITY	Ufficio Filatelico, Governatorato Vatican City
VENEZUELA	Direccion de Correos, Oficina Filatelica Nacional Caracas, Venezuela
WESTERN SAMOA	Philatelic Bureau, GPO Apia, Western Samoa
WEST GERMANY	Versandstelle fur Sammlermarken Postfach 2000

	D-6 Frankfurt 1, Hessen
	West Germany
YEMEN ARAB REPUBLIC	Stamps Bureau, GPO
	San'a', Yemen Arab Republic
YEMEN PEOPLE'S DEMOCRATIC REPUBLIC	Director General of P&T, Postal Division
	Aden, Yemen People's Democratic Republic
YUGOSLAVIA	Biro za Postanske Marke
	Palmoticeva 2
	Belgrade, Yugoslavia
ZAÏRE	Agences Philateliques Gouvernementales
	868 Chaussee de Waterloo
	1180 Brussels, Belgium
ZAMBIA	Philatelic Bureau
	P.O. Box 1857
	Ndola, Zambia

Thecan be no such thing as a definitive listing of collectible stamp topics, for several reasons. A major one is that there have been simply too many subjects treated on the 200,000 or so existing stamps to make it practical for anyone to classify and itemize them all. There is also too much overlapping in subject matter; as a random example, the U.S. Army issue of 1945 (934), showing American forces marching on the Champs Élysées in Paris with the Arc de Triomphe in the background and escorted by a group of planes, has several topical possibilities: warfare, armed forces, peace, famous structures, aircraft, cities, parades—whatever the collector sees, actually. Almost any stamp with an illustration has this multitopic characteristic.

Often, too, a secondary topic may be completely overlooked in listings, especially if it seems unrelated to the stamp's main topics. The Canada issue of 1969 commemorating the outstanding Canadian physician Sir William Osler (495), while an obvious and important addition to almost any medically oriented list, may be unlikely to find its way onto a list of snake stamps; yet a snake is unmistakably present as part of the caduceus—medicine's emblem—on the stamp.

Finally, the facts that a collector can devise his own topic and that no two collectors necessarily see the same elements in a stamp design mean that to a large extent the only thing that really decides the collectibility of a topic is whether or not there are enough stamps dealing with it to make a significant showing. So what this all adds up to is that any topical listing is only a starting point for the collector's own imagination.

In planning a topical collection it should also be remembered that Americana material by no means appears exclusively on U.S. stamps, or Canadiana exclusively on Canadian stamps. For example, a John F. Kennedy collection could embrace hundreds of foreign stamps—but through 1980 only one U.S. stamp. This situation exists for many national topics; none is confined perforce to the stamps of its particular country.

To prevent excessive repetition many subtopics have been omitted from the following list, which as it is— although comprising only a representative cross-sampling of secondary topics—contains almost 275 entries. Some of the omissions have to do with people; it's left understood that in such topics such as anthropology, government, and industry, to name a few, there are commemorated anthropologists, government officials, and industrialists—and each of these groups of people is a collectible subtopic.

There are also many topics common in the animal and vegetable kingdoms that are not shown here. One frequent specialization is by region or habitat—the trees of North America, say, or European songbirds, African wildlife, mountain flora. In the case of animals especially, it's additionally prevalent to collect only a single species; deer, elephants, and the big cats have appeared on stamps many times—and so of course have all domestic animals. Only a few of these subtopics appear in the list below.

The broad general topics, those that lend themselves to division into several subtopics, are shown here in capital letters, with subtopics and more narrowly defined topics in small letters. An asterisk after a listing means that packets of that topic's stamps—some of them containing as many as 1,000 different—are readily available either from local dealers or from mail-order packet dealers. And a number in parentheses after a listing indicates the topic's early-1979 standing in popularity among the top thirty, as determined from a survey of national collector societies, local clubs, and dealers specializing in topical stamps.

AGRICULTURE
airplanes
airships

castles*
cathedrals*
cats*
charity
CHILDREN*
children's art
chemistry
CHRISTMAS (16)
churches*
Sir Winston Churchill
churchmen
cities
classical structures
coats of arms*
coins
colleges and universities
Christopher Columbus
commercial aviation
commercial fishing
COMMUNICATIONS
composers
coniferous trees
CONSERVATION
COSTUMES*
country fairs

dairy industry
dams
DANCING
deciduous trees
dinosaurs
dogs* (19)
domestic animals

EDUCATION
educators
electricity
ENERGY
ENGINEERING
ENTERTAINMENT
EUROPA*
European Economic Community
EXPLORATION
explorers
EXPOSITIONS

factories
fairy tales*
FAMOUS PERSONS (17)
famous structures
farming
festivals
fiction characters
FINE ARTS* (9)
FISH*
FLAGS*
FLOWERS* (11)
folk art
folk dancing
folk dress
folklore
FOOD
food fish
food growing
forestry
Freemasonry
freshwater fish

game animals
game birds
game fish
GEOGRAPHY
geology
GOVERNMENT
government buildings
grain
Great Lakes

HANDICRAFTS
heads of state
HEALTH
health organizations
the heavens
helicopters
heraldry
HISTORY
holidays
horses*
THE HUMANITIES

INDUSTRY
INSECTS* (18)
international organizations
international trade
inventions
inventors
islands

Jesus Christ
journalism
JUDAICA
justice

John F. Kennedy*

LABOR
lakes*
landmarks
LAW
League of Nations
legends
libraries
LITERATURE (24)
logging

Madonnas
manufacturing
maps*
marine life (30)
masks*
mathematicians
MEDICINE (5)
meteorology
MILITARY
military aviation
military honors
minerals
mining
money
monuments
moon shots
motherhood
motion pictures

212

mountains*
museums
MUSIC* (8)
musical instruments
musical performers
mythology

national flowers (29)
national parks
natural history
naval battles
naval forces
news events
newspapers
Nobel Prize winners
nursing*

ocean fish
oceans*
oil drilling
OLYMPIC GAMES*

painters
paintings* (10)
PAN-AMERICANA
PARKS
PEACE
peasants
PEOPLES OF THE WORLD
PETROLEUM INDUSTRY
pharmacology
philosophy
photography
physicians
physics
playwrights
poetry
poets
police
POLITICS
prehistoric animals
printing
PUBLIC BUILDINGS

railroad locomotives
RAILROADS* (7)
Red Cross*
RELIGION* (14)
religious art
REPTILES
rivers*
Franklin D. and Eleanor Roosevelt
roses*
royal jubilees
royalty

sailing ships (27)
sailors
saints
schools
SCIENCE
SCOUTING* (28)
sculpture
sea birds
sea shells*
SHIPS* (3)
slogans
snakes
social reform
soldiers
songbirds
SPACE* (1)
spectator sports
SPORTS* (6)
sports competitions
stained glass
STAMPS* (15)
statesmen
steamships
summer sports

telegraph
telephone
textiles
theater
tourist attractions
toys

214

trains*
TRANSPORTATION* (26)
treaties
TREES
trucks and tractors
tunnels

undersea vessels
uniforms
United Nations (21)

volcanoes

WARFARE
warriors*
warships
waterfalls*
water sports
welfare
wildflowers
WILDLIFE*
winter sports
WOMEN (23)
workers
world's fairs
World War I
World War II
writers

yachting

Index

See section 2, "User's Guide," (pp. 13–45)

for complete alphabetical and category indexes